The USA
1917-1980

Nigel
Smith

Oxford University Press

Oxford University Press
Great Clarendon Street, Oxford OX2 6DP

Oxford New York
Athens Auckland Bangkok Bogota Buenos Aires
Calcutta Cape Town Chennai Dar es Salaam
Delhi Florence Hong Kong Istanbul Karachi
Kuala Lumpur Madrid Melbourne Mexico City
Mumbai Nairobi Paris Sao Paulo Singapore
Taipei Tokyo Toronto Warsaw

and associated companies in
Berlin Ibadan

Oxford is a trade mark of Oxford University Press

© Oxford University Press 1996
First published 1996
Reprinted 1996, 1997 (twice), 1998

ISBN 0 19 917249 8

Printed in Hong Kong

To my parents

The author wishes to acknowledge the assistance of many
US government agencies including the FBI, Bureau of the
Census, Department of State and the Library of Congress.
He is also grateful for the support of his wife, Angela, and
the staff and pupils of Hall Mead School, Upminster.

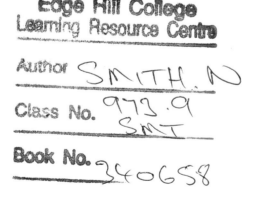

Acknowledgements

The publishers would like to thank the following
for permission to reproduce photographs:

The Advertising Archives p.66 (bottom);
Bettmann Archive pp.30, 70 (bottom), 71;
BFI Stills, Posters and Designs p.14 (top) ©
1930 Turner Entertainment Co. All rights
reserved; Colorific/Black Star pp.93 (centre –
Ray Cranbourne), 94 (James Pickerell), 102
(John Launois), 115 (Dennis Brack); John
Hillelson Agency p.26 (top); Hulton Deutsch
Collection pp.6, 51 (bottom), 58, 83 (bottom),
104 (top), 112 (left), 114, 117 (bottom), 119;
/Bettmann Archive 17 (bottom), 20 (centre), 32,
37, 52, 56, 70 (top); Imperial War Museum pp 7,
9, 43, 51 (top); Library of Congress p.40;
Magnum pp.69 (P. Jones Griffiths), 85 (bottom –
Larry Schiller), 92 (Bruno Barbey); Mansell pp.10
(right), 45 (bottom); Mirror Syndication
International pp.25, 36, 39, 42, 66 (top);
National Museum of American Art, Washington,
D.C./Art Resource, NY p.26 (bottom); Peter
Newark's Pictures pp.8 (both), 12 (bottom right),
15, 18, 24, 28, 40 (top), 45 (top), 46, 47, 48, 49
(top), 50, 67, 78, 95, 100; Office of War
Information/F.D. Roosevelt Library p.34;
Portland Oregonian p.93 (top – cartoon by
Brimrose); Popperfoto pp.19, 53 (bottom), 55,
61, 72, 75 (both) 79, 84 (both), 87, 97, 99, 104
(left), 107 (bottom), 112 (right), 117 (top);
Range/Bettmann/UPI pp.83 (top), 85 (top), 96,
106, 107 (centre), 111 (bottom), 116 (bottom);
Redferns p.103 (both – Elliott Landy);
REX Features p.80; RFE/RL Research Institute,
Munich p.59; Franklin D. Roosevelt Library
pp.31, 38 (bottom); School of Slavonic and East
European Studies, University of London p.65;
Nigel Smith pp.10 (left), 11, 14 (bottom), 20
(bottom), 35, 38 (top), 41, 63; Topham Picture
Source pp.53 (top), 76, 82; TRH p.111 (top);
Harry S. Truman Library p.54; The Washington
Post p.60; Whitney Museum of American Art
p.13;

Front cover: Bridgeman Art Library; Rex Features

All illustrations are by Jeff Edwards

Contents

*I*ntroduction

Twentieth-century American history topics will continue to be popular topics at GCSE. America, with its great geographical and ethnic diversity is a fascinating subject for study. Given the enormous impact of the USA, for better or worse, on all our lives, it is particularly appropriate that pupils should study some modern American history in their senior years.

This book traces the main events and historical trends between 1917, when the population was just over 101 million and evenly divided between rural and urban, and 1980, by which time there were 200 million people of whom 70% lived in the cities. During that time America abandoned her reluctance to play any part in world affairs and became a superpower determined to dominate in our world in what some have called the 'arrogance of power'. Pupils will not only learn how that came about but will have plenty of opportunities to weigh the evidence and assess the arguments over America's changed international role as well as the changes in the lives of her people. Although, increasingly, the 'American Dream' has appeared flawed, the USA remains a nation of vitality and excitement. It will be a strange pupil who finds nothing of interest in this course.

Teachers, mindful of the importance of developing economic awareness and an understanding of citizenship, will find plenty of scope to put current issues and problems into perspective. There are a wide variety of sources, documents and illustrations intended to stimulate classroom discussion and to enable pupils to work on a number of topics including issues of race and gender that have contemporary as well as historical significance.

The text is appropriate for the average attaining pupil whilst providing ample opportunity for those higher attainers to prepare for and demonstrate their achievement. The tasks scattered throughout the text provide the opportunity to test knowledge and skills and to prepare pupils for GCSE examinations. Some tasks are definitely suitable to be used for 'coursework' assignments. Many of the exercises allow for differentiated responses. The text, documentary sources and illustrations will motivate pupils, many of whom will wish to research deeper into specific topics than is possible within a single textbook. In particular, reading more thoroughly about the many individuals only briefly mentioned here will prove rewarding. For some pupils this work will lead to further study of the USA at A Level and, who knows, at graduate level, where not only straightforward American history is offered but also courses in American Studies are available.

Nigel Smith

1 *T*he USA and the First World War

The USA in 1917

Americans had many reasons to feel satisfied with the achievements of their nation by 1917. The wilderness of a few years earlier had been replaced by towns, farms and railroads, and in the early years of the twentieth century roads for the growing number of motor cars began to link every part of the country. The standard of living rose steadily. By 1917 the USA was the world's pre-eminent industrial nation, both producing and consuming 70% of the world's oil. Across the great plains of the Midwest huge and efficient farms grew 30% of the world's wheat and 75% of the corn, and swamped European markets with vast quantities of cheap food.

Apart from the Native American Indians, every other American was either an immigrant or a descendant of people who had emigrated in pursuit of the 'American dream' of freedom, opportunity and prosperity. America needed immigrants to settle the prairies, construct the railroads, and build up and operate the new industries, and in the process created a vibrant, multi-cultural and powerful nation. During the years 1900–1920 more than fourteen million immigrants landed in America to increase the rapidly expanding population to more than 106 million. The 'Old immigration' from the 1820s until the 1880s came predominantly from northern Europe. By 1917 their children had created first and second generations proud of their roots but committed to an ideal of America shaped by their own background and beliefs. They were largely white Anglo-Saxon Protestants ('WASP'). But the 'New immigration' after 1880, and especially the rush of immigrants 1900–1914, were mainly poor and illiterate people from eastern and southern Europe who were held in some contempt by many older established Americans. Assimilation was

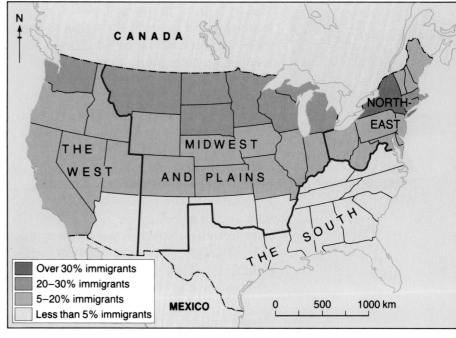

difficult for these new arrivals. There was no more free land available for farming so many of them settled in crowded city neighbourhoods with people from their own country, where they continued to speak their native language and follow their traditional culture. By 1917 the population was almost evenly divided between those who lived in rural communities and the urban dwellers. But it was in the cities that the population was increasing most rapidly, accompanied by social problems such as poor housing and crime.

In addition, there were the descendants of the unwilling immigrants forcibly taken to the Americas as slaves. Slavery had been ended by the bitter Civil War (1861–65), but black Americans suffered discrimination in the northern states and the indignity of segregation in the South, by which they were denied equal rights and opportunities. In the 'land of the free' these 10.5 million people (in 1920) were amongst the poorest in the nation and had virtually no political say in how their country was governed.

The distribution of European immigrants in the USA in 1914

President Woodrow
Wilson

In 1912 Woodrow Wilson, the candidate of the Democratic Party, was elected President. His manifesto, the New Freedom programme, was aimed at the 'common man', such as labourers, farmers and white people in the southern states. Wilson believed in strong presidential leadership and government action to solve social and economic problems. But, unwilling to antagonise white voters, Wilson did nothing to stop racial segregation. Gradually the Democrats created a rather uneasy alliance of urban Catholic voters in the northern cities and the poorer rural voters in the South. The alternative party, the Republican Party, often known as the 'GOP' (Grand Old Party) advocated laissez-faire policies with only limited action by the federal (central) government and more power in the hands of local governments in each of the forty-eight states. Republican support after 1912 came increasingly from 'WASP' Americans, especially in the northern and some western states.

Neutrality

From Neutrality to War

On 2 April 1917 the United States of America declared war on Germany. To Americans as well as Europeans it was the 'Great War'. Since August 1914 Europe had been engulfed by the greatest and costliest conflict that had ever taken place. At the start of the war the American President, Woodrow Wilson, had argued that the USA should remain neutral and not become involved in Europe's 'Civil War'. In 1916 Wilson, a Democrat, was re-elected for a second term with the campaign slogan, 'He kept us out of the war'.

At first American public opinion was firmly on the side of neutrality. Most Americans had little or no interest in world affairs and supported a policy of isolationism. America, they believed, had no reason to become involved in the arguments of other nations. Wilson also knew that many Americans had no sympathy with Britain: Irish Americans disliked Britain because of the way she ruled Ireland, whilst millions of German Americans wanted a German victory. Then there were Russian Jews who had fled to the USA and were eager for the Germans to defeat the hated Russian Tsar. At the start of the war, President Wilson is said to have told the German Ambassador, 'We have to be neutral. Otherwise, our mixed populations would wage war on each other'. In 1914, on the outbreak of the war in Europe, Wilson advocated what became known as 'determined neutrality'.

No single event or factor destroyed this neutrality and led to America entering the war on the side of Britain and her allies. American opinion had increasingly turned against the Germans as they stepped up submarine attacks on shipping, including passenger vessels crossing the Atlantic Ocean. The sinking of the British ship, the *Lusitania*, in May 1915, aroused great anger as 128 Americans were among the 1198 passengers who perished. Further attacks followed until the German government announced in June 1915 that passenger ships would not be sunk without warning.

There is no doubt that President Wilson's personal sympathies were with Britain. The USA and Britain had very considerable economic links, and a German victory would have been financially very damaging. By early 1917, the USA had loaned the Allies two billion dollars and many American factories had become dependent upon Allied purchases of war equipment.

In January 1917, the Germans decided to return to a policy of unrestricted submarine attacks on shipping. On 3 February, an American liner was sunk, and Wilson responded immediately by breaking off diplomatic relations with Germany.

> Property can be paid for, but the lives of peaceful and innocent people cannot be. The present German submarine warfare against commerce is warfare against mankind.

 B President Wilson in a message to the Congress in January 1917

Another incident infuriated Americans against the Germans. In January 1917, the German Foreign Minister, Alfred Zimmermann, sent orders to the German Ambassador in Mexico that he should try to enlist Mexican support against the USA. In return, Mexico was offered the opportunity to regain territory, supposedly theirs, that was now part of the USA. The Zimmermann note was intercepted by the British secret service and its publication in March 1917 outraged Americans.

 C The Zimmermann note

Berlin, January 19, 1917
On the first of February we intend to begin submarine warfare unrestricted. In spite of this it is our intention to keep neutral the United States of America. If this attempt is not successful, we propose an alliance on the following basis with Mexico: That we shall make war together and together make peace... it is understood that Mexico is to reconquer their lost territory in New Mexico, Texas and Arizona... the employment of ruthless submarine warfare now promises to compel England to make peace in a few months.

Zimmermann

The Zimmermann note and the refusal of the Germans to stop their attacks on neutral American shipping was clear evidence of German aggression, and helped Wilson to overcome any objections to America entering the war. On 2 April 1917, less than a month after the publication of the Zimmermann note, Wilson went to Congress to demand a declaration of war against Germany.

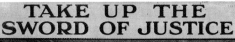

 D This British poster was intended to remind Americans that 128 US citizens had lost their lives in the sinking of the *Lusitania* and to urge them to join the Allies in the war against Germany

 E War

Vessels of every kind, whatever their flag, their character, their cargo, their destination, their errand, have been ruthlessly sent to the bottom without warning and without thought of help or mercy for those on board, the vessels of friendly neutrals along with those of belligerents. Even hospital ships and ships carrying relief to the sorely bereaved and stricken people of Belgium... Neutrality is no longer feasible or desirable where the peace of the world is involved and the freedom of its peoples, and the menace to that peace and freedom lies in the existence of autocratic government backed by organised force which is controlled wholly by their will, not by the will of their people... The world must be made safe for democracy. Its peace must be planted upon the tested foundations of political liberty. We have no selfish ends to serve, we desire no conquest, no dominion...
... It is a fearful thing to lead this great peaceful people into war, into the most terrible and disastrous of all wars, civilization itself seeming to be in the balance.

Part of President Wilson's speech to Congress explaining to the people why America had to go to war

1 Explain the reasons behind President Wilson's policy of 'determined neutrality'.
2 What were the causes that led the USA to enter the war in 1917?

America at War

> ...a war for freedom and justice and self-government amongst all the nations of the world... the German people themselves included.

This was Wilson's explanation in 1917 of what he believed the real purpose of the war to be

America's decision to fight was the turning point in the First World War. But the USA was ill prepared for the war that President Wilson had tried so hard to avoid. Although the decision to declare war was not challenged, there was little enthusiasm for the conflict. The horrors of trench warfare with high casualties along the Western Front were well known and, understandably, many young men of military age were reluctant to go half-way across the world to risk their lives in a European war, the origins of which few Americans understood.

From the start, Wilson's approach to the war differed from the aims of the leaders of Britain and France. Wilson argued that the purpose of the war was not solely to defeat German aggression, but also to accomplish the liberation of the German nation from an autocratic government based on force. Britain and France, however, were determined to destroy Germany forever as a dominant power in Europe.

3 How did President Wilson's intentions in fighting differ from his allies?

The US military contribution to the war was very significant, and proved crucial in revitalising Allied armies along the Western Front. In the seventeen months before the Armistice, almost five million Americans were mobilised and 53,513 were killed in action, together with 204,002 wounded.

In July 1918 American troops helped save Paris from a German advance. The US Army in France, led by General Pershing, moved against the Germans on the southern front and, by the end of September, a million and a quarter American soldiers were fighting in France. The exhausted German armies lacked the reserves of men and equipment necessary to continue fighting, and at 11am on the 11th of November 1918 the First World War ended with the Armistice.

Gee I wish I were a man

The US Navy played a crucial part in the war by defending convoys against German U-Boat attacks, as huge quantities of supplies and soldiers were transported to Europe

Uncle Sam at War

Patriotic appeals such as this were not enough to raise sufficient troops to take part in a war more than three thousand miles from American homes, and young men had to be conscripted to serve in the armed forces

American soldiers from a balloon observation unit in France in 1918

The Fourteen Points

4 How significant was the US participation in the war?
5 Why did the US government introduce conscription?

The League of Nations

In January 1918, eleven months before the war ended, President Wilson issued his peace proposals in the form of fourteen points which he intended as the basis of a lasting post-war peace settlement.

1 There should be no more secret treaties.
2 Absolute freedom of the seas at all times.
3 Free trade between nations.
4 All armaments to be reduced.
5 The rights and opinions of people living in colonies to be considered when settling colonial claims.
6 The Germans must withdraw from Russian territory.
7 Belgium must be free and independent.
8 France will regain the territory of Alsace-Lorraine.
9 The border between Austria and Italy to be readjusted.
10 The peoples of Eastern Europe must have self-determination in their own independent nations.
11 Romania, Serbia, and Montenegro must be liberated and their territory guaranteed by international agreement.
12 The people in the Turkish Empire must decide upon their own future.
13 Poland should be an independent nation with access to the Baltic Sea.
14 An association of nations – the League of Nations – to be set up to settle all disputes between countries.

The key point of the Fourteen Points, was Wilson's proposal for the League of Nations which, by settling disputes peacefully, would prevent any further wars.

Unlike his wartime allies, Wilson had no wish to punish the Germans. The President prided himself on his idealism.

> Sometimes people call me an idealist. Well that is the way I know I am an American. America is the only idealistic nation in the world.

President Wilson in 1919

At the Paris Peace Conference in 1919, Wilson was compelled to sacrifice many of his 'Fourteen Points'. But he succeeded in his determination to include the League of Nations in the Versailles Treaty that was finally imposed on Germany. Wilson's concept was collective security, by which nations would stand together to combat aggression. If one country was attacked then other members of the League would apply sanctions against the aggressor. As a last resort, they could send military assistance. However, the President faced a humiliating rejection of both the League and the Treaty of Versailles by the US Congress.

6 Explain the reasons behind President Wilson's peace proposals?
7 What did Wilson mean by 'collective security'?

Return to isolationism

Now the war was over, many Americans were keen to withdraw once again from world affairs and return to a policy of isolationism. They were afraid that League membership would involve them permanently in the affairs of Europe. Senator Henry Cabot Lodge, leader of the Republican opposition to Wilson, successfully led the campaign against the League. Republicans were hostile to Wilson anyway, but they were also concerned to protect American sovereignty and the freedom to act independently. They argued that the decision to go to war should rest solely with the US Congress and not with the League. Lodge came up with fourteen points of criticism, the 'Lodge Reservations', to match Wilson's 'Fourteen Points' (Source H). Another Republican, Senator Borah, declared he would vote against the League even if Jesus Christ returned to earth to argue in its favour, and many others were just as inflexible.

J Danger of the League

...this League is primarily a political organisation, and I object strongly to having the politics of the United States turn upon disputes where deep feeling is aroused but in which we have no direct interest... I wish to limit strictly our interference in the affairs of Europe and of Africa... the less we undertake to play the part of umpire and thrust ourselves into European conflicts the better for the United States and for the world.

This is part of the speech made by Senator Lodge in August 1919

K 'Seein' Things'

Republicans, known as 'irreconcilables', saw the League as a threat to American independence of action rather than a safeguard for peace

President Wilson refused to compromise and embarked on an exhausting trip across the country to explain his proposals directly to the people.

... mothers who lost their sons in France have come to me... they rightly believe that their sons saved the liberty of the world. They believe that wrapped up with the liberty of the world is the continuous protection of that liberty by the concerted powers of all civilised people. They believe that this sacrifice was made in order that other sons should not be called upon for a similar gift – the gift of life.

On 19 March 1920, the US Senate finally decided that America would not sign the Treaty of Versailles or join the League of Nations. America's refusal to join the League, the brainchild of its own President, weakened the organisation from the start, and was an important reason why it lacked the power to enforce its decisions.

L

A few hours after making this speech at Pueblo, Colorado on 25 September 1919, the President was taken ill. Several days later he suffered a paralysing stroke from which he never properly recovered.

THE GAP IN THE BRIDGE.

M
The League of Nations had a crucial weakness with the USA – the keystone – refusing to join

8 Explain the arguments put forward by supporters of isolationism.
9 Why do you think there was so much support for a return to isolationism?
10 What consequences of American policy might Europeans have regretted? Explain your answer.
11 What are the points that the cartoonists in Sources K and M are making?

Essay:
i Explain the causes and the results of the American involvement in the First World War.
ii 'The world will be absolutely in despair if America deserts it.' Discuss the significance of this comment by President Wilson in 1919.
iii Why did the USA enter the First World War but not the League of Nations?

2 The Twenties

'The Age of Excess'

The experience of war irreversibly changed America. During the 1920s new inventions such as radio, refrigerators and vacuum cleaners, and the mass produced motor car, not only altered the ways of daily life but generated an unprecedented growth in business that established the US economy as predominant in the world. The three Presidents of the 1920s, Harding, Coolidge and Hoover, were all Republicans and represented the views of business and the Wall Street stock market. The Republican Party was against any idea of a welfare state or government regulation of business. It was President Harding, elected in 1920, who coined the slogan, 'Return to Normalcy'. But the boom of the 1920s with its new music and dances, the disregarding of sexual inhibitions together with new and sometimes immodest fashions, and the growth of organised crime and some outrageous political scandals, meant the country was far removed from the normal way of life prior to 1917.

'The business of America'

'The chief business of America is business', declared Calvin Coolidge, who became President in 1923 after the sudden death of Harding. He greatly admired businessmen and firmly adhered to a 'laissez-faire' policy with as few federal government restrictions as possible on business. He felt private enterprise capitalism should be left alone to produce wealth and profits. The *Wall Street Journal*, a financial newspaper, approvingly declared: 'Never before, here or anywhere else, has a government been so completely fused with business'.

Which businesses flourished

The growth of industrial production, jobs, profits, wages, and the standard of living, during the years 1920–1929 was impressive. A policy of strict tariff barriers, known as 'protectionism', restricted the entry of foreign imports so that they could not compete with American-produced goods. The USA had sufficient raw materials as well as workers to satisfy demand for new products. The Americans' love affair with the automobile deepened as mass production, pioneered by Henry Ford, brought prices down and created huge numbers of well paid jobs on the production lines. Around 1914 a Ford Model T cost $850, but by 1926 the price had fallen to just $295, and it even had a self-starter. And all the time Ford made huge profits. By 1929 Americans owned more than twenty-three million cars, compared with seven million ten years earlier. A massive programme of road construction, together with gas stations, hotels and roadside diners, provided further employment. Other huge new industries expanded rapidly, including the development of electrical power to drive factory machinery, to light the streets in the growing cities, and to power the new appliances such as vacuum cleaners and refrigerators. JC Penney department stores increased in number from 312 in 1920 to 1395 by 1929. Piggly Wiggly introduced what was to become another American institution, the supermarket. The infant industry of advertising grew into a major business with the task of promoting the new products, and developed new techniques including the movie houses and commercial radio. The sponsorship of afternoon radio series by soap companies gave rise to the term 'soap opera'.

Production of Motor Vehicles 1921–1929
(Source: US Dept of Commerce)

1921	1,682,000
1922	2,646,000
1923	4,180,000
1924	3,738,000
1925	4,428,000
1926	4,506,000
1927	3,580,000
1928	4,601,000
1929	5,622,000

This slogan was used by Calvin Coolidge in the 1924 election. A man of few words, he was totally committed to the free-enterprise system that appeared to be so successful during his presidency.

The Ten-Millionth Ford

The 10,000,000th Ford car left the Highland Park factories of the Ford Motor Company June 4. This is a production achievement unapproached in automotive history. Tremendous volume has been the outgrowth of dependable, convenient, economical service.

Ford Motor Company Detroit, Michigan

SEE THE NEAREST AUTHORIZED FORD DEALER

The Touring Car
$295
F.O.B. Detroit

B

More than any other single product the automobile transformed everyday life in a country where great distances separated cities and millions lived in remote rural communities. The advertising industry helped make people feel dissatisfied if they did not own the new products and models rolling off the production lines.

C Gross National Product
(Source: US Dept. of Commerce)

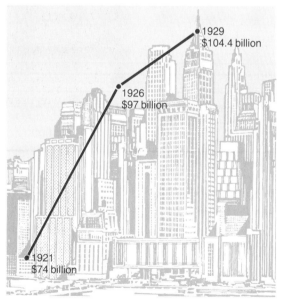

1929
$104.4 billion

1926
$97 billion

1921
$74 billion

In March 1929 Herbert Hoover succeeded Coolidge as President. A few months earlier, during his election campaign, he expressed great satisfaction in the American economy and the years of Republican government.

D Prosperity

We have increased in home ownership, we have expanded the investment of the average man... Today there are almost 9 automobiles for every 10 families, where 7$\frac{1}{2}$ years ago only enough automobiles were running to average less than 4 for every 10 families. The slogan of progress is changing from the full dinner pail to the full garage. Our people have more to eat, better things to wear, and better homes... Wages have increased, the cost of living has decreased. The job of every man and woman has been made more secure. We have in this short period decreased the fear of poverty, the fear of unemployment, the fear of old age... In 7$\frac{1}{2}$ years we have added 70% to the electric power at the elbow of our workers and further promoted them from carriers of burdens to directors of machines. We have steadily reduced the sweat in human labour. Our hours of labour are lessened; our leisure has increased... In these 7$\frac{1}{2}$ years the radio has brought music and laughter, education and political discussion to almost every fireside.

Herbert Hoover speaking during his campaign for the Presidency in New York City on 22 October 1928. At his inauguration, Hoover declared that he had no fears for the future of the country.

1 What use are the statistics in Sources A and C, to an historian?

President Hoover giving his inaugural address in 1929

The Jazz age

Although many people were thrilled by the increased prosperity, they were not always so keen on some of its results. The mass consumption economy produced new popular music promoted by movies, radio and records. Jazz emerged onto the national scene from its black African-American roots, and parents were horrified by the enthusiasm of their children for this new music with its sexually explicit songs and dances such as the Black Bottom and the Charleston. Some cities, including New York, Cleveland and Detroit, prohibited the public performance of jazz in dance halls, but this only increased its appeal. Just as conservative elders failed to discourage the music, they could not stop the revolution in sexual behaviour either. College students were among the first to abandon many of the inhibitions of their parents and a flood of novels, magazine and newspaper articles, and Hollywood movies, informed the country of this new behaviour. New uses emerged for the mass produced automobiles that Henry Ford had never imagined! For the first time economic prosperity gave young people the opportunity to engage in so-called daring behaviour. Increased smoking was one result; sales of cigarettes doubled during the 1920s. The writer F. Scott Fitzgerald called it, 'the age of excess'. It was very difficult for parents who had grown up in the much more restrictive age of the chaperone to accept this new morality and it must have led to many family arguments.

The new music and behaviour was reflected in dramatic changes in the fashions worn by younger people. In 1919, women's skirts were usually about six inches above the ground, but by 1927 they were at the knees. The new smart young women of the twenties were nicknamed 'flappers'. Hollywood movies promoted the flappers, and millions of people around the world saw and tried to imitate the fashions and behaviour that went with them.

Actress Joan Crawford was the most famous flapper of them all. She kissed, drank, smoked and danced the Charleston in films such as *Our Modern Maidens* and girls loved it and tried to copy her. To many, the flappers were a clear sign of the decline of traditional standards, whilst to others they were seen as 'new women' in the tradition of American individualism and freedom. Women had gained the right to vote in 1919 and now asserted their right to independence in other ways.

John Sloan. 'Sixth Avenue Elevated At Third Street. 1928. Oil on canvas. 30 × 40 inches. (76.2 cm c 101.6 cm). Collection of Whitney Museum of American Art. Purchase 36.154.

2 What can an historian learn about the changes in daily life during the 1920s from Sources A–F?

3 Source E is a painting. Does this mean that it is of little use to an historian?

4 Do Sources A–E prove that all Americans were better off during the 1920s?

5 Source D is a political speech. How useful is this to an historian?

6 How useful are each of the Sources A–D in proving that the 1920s was a period of economic prosperity?

She doesn't drink,
She doesn't pet,
She hasn't been
To college yet.

This witty rhyme appeared in a college student paper – *The Tennessee Mugwump*

Joan Crawford is doubtless the best example of the flapper, the girl you see at smart night clubs, gowned to the apex of sophistication, toying iced glasses with a remote, faintly bitter expression, dancing deliciously, laughing a great deal, with wide hurt eyes. Young things with a talent for living.

These words were written by F. Scott Fitzgerald, the writer who did so much to capture the spirit of the 1920s and the flappers in tremendously successful books such as *The Great Gatsby*

H

By sheer force of violence, the flapper has established the feminine right to equal representation in such hitherto masculine fields of endeavor as smoking and drinking, swearing, petting and upsetting the community peace.

The New York Times, 1929

 Joan Crawford, a successful Hollywood actress over more than forty years, epitomised flappers in the 1929 silent movie, *Untamed*

 The 'flapper' became the symbol of the 'roaring twenties', as young women enjoyed a freedom their mothers had never known. Young men enjoyed it as well!

Religious revival

Freedom of religion is guaranteed in the USA by the First Amendment to the Constitution, ratified in 1791, which also forbade any kind of established or official Church, and so ensured the separation of Church and State. Many immigrants had fled to America because of religious intolerance in their own countries. Church attendance there has always been far greater than in Britain. In the 1920s there was a revival of religious conservatism amongst those Christians who supported fundamentalist ideas, such as a rigid belief in the literal truth of the Bible. They angrily challenged modern approaches to Christianity. Protestant fundamentalism was particularly prevalent in rural areas, especially the South and Midwest, which became known as the 'Bible Belt' and where open hostility was shown towards those who did not share these views.

In 1925 a clash occurred between the two sides, which highlighted both the intolerance and influence of some fundamentalists. That year the Tennessee legislature made the teaching of Darwin's theory of evolution illegal, because it contradicted the Bible's literal explanation of the Creation. The climax to the argument, which had raged for some time, came when this law was challenged by the American Civil Liberties Union (ACLU) in Dayton Tennessee in what was colloquially called the 'monkey trial'. John Scopes, a schoolteacher, represented by a distinguished Chicago lawyer, Clarence Dayton, was opposed by a fundamentalist leader, William Jennings Bryan, a lawyer who had three times been the unsuccessful Democratic candidate for the presidency. The arguments between the two lawyers were fierce and just as bitter as the division between the fundamentalists and their critics. To many people outside the Bible Belt, the fundamentalist ideas were shown by the trial to be foolish, but Scopes was found guilty, which indeed he was, of teaching the theory of evolution. Bryan who had described the trial as a 'duel to the death' died quite suddenly a few days after its conclusion.

Fundamentalists were keen supporters of prohibition (see chapter 3) and many were Klansmen (see chapter 4). In spite of their traditional support for the Democratic Party, they helped to defeat the Democratic candidate, Al Smith, in 1928, because he came from New York City, was a Roman Catholic and opposed prohibition.

Poverty in the midst of plenty

Although the American economy was booming, not everybody shared in the affluence. Six million families – 42% of the total – had an income of less than $1000 a year and certainly could not afford the new cars and gadgets rolling off the production lines. Presidents Coolidge and Hoover advocated a policy of 'rugged individualism' that basically meant 'every man for himself', with no welfare support from the government for the poor.

Agriculture, which only a few years earlier had been the largest industry, suffered a serious decline in the 1920s as farm prices fell to the advantage of the consumer, and led to widespread foreclosures, especially in the South.

> I confess I was not prepared for what I actually saw. It seemed almost incredible that such conditions of poverty could really exist.

Fiorello La Guardia, a Congressman from East Harlem, New York City, 1928

> ...prosperity was concentrated at the top. While from 1922 to 1929 real wages in manufacturing went up per capita 1.4% a year, the holders of common stocks gained 16.4% a year... One-tenth of 1% of the families at the top received as much income as 42% of the families at the bottom... Every year in the 1920s, about 25,000 workers were killed on the job and 100,000 permanently disabled. Two million people in New York City lived in tenements condemned as firetraps.

Howard Zinn, *A People's History of the United States*, 1980

K Whilst industry was booming during the 1920s, agriculture was weak and many farmers were forced to sell their farms

Freedom

Although there appeared to be new freedom in social behaviour in the 1920s, how much freedom in politics and expression actually existed? A wave of strikes and accompanying violence after the First World War caused great alarm. The Russian Revolution in 1917 had established the first Communist state (which the USA refused to recognise until 1933) supposedly committed to spreading revolution against capitalism worldwide. Those who supported Socialist or Communist ideas, particularly in trade union activities, were harrassed by local police departments as well as by the Federal Justice Department. During the so-called 'Red Scare' 4000 men and women, many of them recent immigrants, were rounded up on New Years Day 1920 for allegedly subversive activities. Most of them were innocent but 600 aliens were deported. Under this pressure, union membership fell from over 6 million in 1920 to about 3.6 million in 1923 and union effectiveness declined even more.

The most controversial episode was the case of Sacco and Vanzetti. On 5 May 1920 these two Italian-born anarchists, Nicola Sacco and Bartolomeo Vanzetti, were charged in Massachusetts with murdering two men during an armed robbery. They protested their innocence and claimed they were being persecuted for their well known political beliefs. The judge in the case privately called them 'those anarchist bastards' and they were found guilty and sentenced to death. In spite of serious doubts and a massive worldwide campaign they were executed in the electric chair in 1927.

Old and new immigration 1891–1920

Low steamship fares gave the poorer classes in Europe the opportunity to emigrate to the United States

Immigration: white Protestants only

A combination of racism and religious prejudice, fear of overcrowding in some cities, and also of Socialist political ideas flooding in from Europe, resulted in a restrictive quota system being set up in 1921 to end the great migration to the USA. It was a victory for those 'WASPs' who had little respect for the southern and eastern Europeans who formed the bulk of immigrants 1900–1920. The declared intention of the quota system was:
 i to reduce immigration and allow assimilation of those already in the USA;
 ii to preserve a reasonable degree of homogeneity in the US population.
Under the quota system, based on national origins, four-fifths of those allowed to enter came from Britain and Ireland, Germany, Holland, Switzerland and Scandinavia. However, few if any were permitted from southern European countries, and none at all from East Asia. Most new immigrants after 1921 were, therefore, white and Protestant, which was, after all, the whole idea.

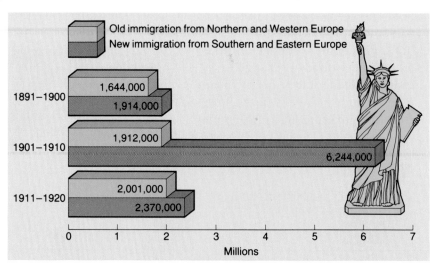

Old immigration from Northern and Western Europe
New immigration from Southern and Eastern Europe

Period	Old	New
1891–1900	1,644,000	1,914,000
1901–1910	1,912,000	6,244,000
1911–1920	2,001,000	2,370,000

Millions

7 How reliable are Sources I–K?
8 With reference to all the Sources, explain how they provide a balanced picture of America in the 1920s.
9 'The prosecution of John Scopes was an attack on civil liberties.' Assess the validity of that view.
10 Which groups of people might not have agreed with the idea of 'rugged individualism'?
11 With reference to Source L, explain the real purpose and effect of the quota system for immigration.
Essay: Does the term 'Roaring Twenties' accurately describe America, 1920–1929?
Further research: How can novels such as those by F. Scott Fitzgerald and Sinclair Lewis help historians understand life in the 1920s?

3 Prohibition
'The noble experiment'

The prohibition of the manufacture or sale of all alcoholic drinks anywhere in the USA between 1920 and 1933 was a well intentioned but disastrously flawed social experiment. For many years organisations such as the Anti-Saloon League had been campaigning for a total legal ban on alcoholic drink. The Anti-Saloon League became a very effective and powerful pressure group as it mobilised the Churches and exercised considerable political influence that helped elect many 'dry' (as supporters of prohibition were known) politicians to the US Congress. Most support for prohibition came from the small towns and rural areas where Protestant churches had considerable congregations who were critical of the standards of behaviour and morality in the northern cities such as New York and Chicago. The argument over prohibition reflected the division that existed between rural and urban America. Alcohol and drunkenness were seen as the root of many evils including crime, sexual immorality and poverty. So strong was the campaign that even many 'wets' who enjoyed a drink were unwilling to publicly oppose the Anti-Saloon League, and politicians were reluctant to oppose prohibition for fear of losing votes.

On 16 January 1920 the Eighteenth Amendment to the US Constitution, together with the Volstead Act, banned the 'manufacture, sale, or transport of intoxicating liquors', which were defined as having more than 0.5 per cent alcohol. But there was little chance that millions of Americans would simply give up drinking beer, wine and whisky, just because there was a law against it. Many people were ready to seize the opportunity to supply alcoholic drink and so make huge profits. Prohibition, intended in part to reduce crime, instead helped to produce a huge crime wave. According to President Hoover,

prohibition was 'a noble experiment' but its failings and the difficulties of enforcement were obvious from the start. In many places, including the nation's capital, it did not even reduce drunkenness.

1 What arguments were put forward in support of prohibition?
2 Why was the Anti-Saloon League so successful in 1919?
3 What point is being made in the poster, Source C?

A

Bad effects of alcoholic drink:
● damage to health
● increased poverty
● crime and violence
● absenteeism and reduced production

B Washington DC arrests for drunkenness

| 1919 | 3565 |
| 1923 | 9149 |

C

The Anti-Saloon League, a very effective pressure group, warned that alcoholic drink threatened the future prosperity and strength of America

This 1922 photograph shows an illegal 500 gallon whisky still seized in Washington DC, not far from the President's White House

The OVERSHADOWING CURSE
THE LEGALIZED SALOON

HAS SHE A FAIR CHANCE?

"Our religion demands that every child should have a fair chance for citizenship in the coming Kingdom. Our patriotism demands a saloonless country and a stainless flag."—P. A. Baker, General Superintendent Anti-Saloon League of America.

Organised crime

Organised crime set up a massive alternative industry producing and distributing illegal drink. Bootleggers, as those who supplied illicit drink were nicknamed, smuggled huge quantities across the thousands of miles of border between Canada and the USA; from the British islands of the Bahamas to Florida; and across the US-Mexico border. Others operated countless illegal breweries and stills. Thousands of speakeasies, the name given to illegal bars, opened up across the country. By 1925 it was estimated there were 100,000 speakeasies in New York City alone. Bribery and intimidation protected them from the local police and politicians or from rival criminal gangs. Many of them operated almost openly and often, as in Chicago, with the connivance of both the local police and the Mayor.

Prohibition alone did not cause organised crime, but it did give the criminals a wonderful opportunity for expansion. The most notorious of the racketeers and gang leaders was Al Capone in Chicago. He employed new methods of murder, extortion and intimidation in gaining and maintaining his control over all forms of vice, including gambling and brothels as well as the speakeasies. Capone, with his expensive suits, bulletproof Cadillac, and generous support for Chicago charities, was a well known figure who liked to keep company with celebrities and politicians, including the city's corrupt Mayor, 'Big Bill' Thompson. In 1927 it is estimated that his empire of illegal activities produced an income of $27 million. Capone described himself as a businessman supplying the public with what they wanted.

D Breaking the law

...one cannot make a crime overnight out of something that millions of people have never regarded as a crime... Slaking thirst became a cherished personal liberty, and many ardent wets (those opposed to prohibition) believed that the way to bring about repeal was to violate the law on a large enough scale... The old-time 'men-only' corner saloons were replaced by thousands of 'speakeasies', with their tiny grilled window through which the thirsty spoke softly before the barred door was opened. Women frequented such dives. Hard liquor, especially the cocktail, was drunk in staggering volume by both sexes... 'home brew' and 'bathtub gin' became popular... The worst of the homemade 'rotgut' produced blindness, even death. The affable bootlegger worked in silent partnership with the friendly undertaker.

T. A. Bailey & D. M. Kennedy, *The American Pageant*, 1979.

E Al Capone

What's Al Capone done, then? He's supplied a legitimate demand. Some call it bootlegging. Some call it racketeering. I call it business. They say I violate the prohibition law. Who doesn't?

Al Capone in 1927 defending his criminal activities (quoted in G.B. Tindall and D.E. Shi, *America*, 1992).

 A police 'mug shot' of Al (Scarface) Capone, the King of Chicago's mobsters during the years of prohibition

4 What were some of the consequences of prohibition?

5 Why were many normally law-abiding citizens prepared to break the prohibition laws?

F
The cold blooded murders in the 'St Valentine's Day Massacre' brutally demonstrated the violence of those behind the speakeasies, and people were shocked by the increasing shootings and gang warfare that apppeared to have resulted from prohibition

But Capone's profits depended on violence against all those who stood in his way, whether they were honest police officers trying to uphold the law or rival gangsters. Capone ordered the executions of those who refused to accede to his demands, and he effectively controlled both the Mayor and the police. Capone is thought to have been behind most of the one hundred and thirty murders in Chicago in 1926–27, although not a single murderer was convicted. But in 1929 the most spectacular and shocking event of the prohibition era occurred, which finally brought home to people the fact that the trade in illegal drink was closely linked to violent crime. Several members of one of Capone's rival gangs, led by Bugs Moran, were killed. Moran himself only narrowly avoided being slaughtered. Known as the St Valentine's Day Massacre, the murderers, disguised as police officers, machine-gunned seven of Moran's gang members. Although Capone was down in Florida with a perfect alibi, it was widely believed that he had ordered the execution. Capone was never convicted of any offence of violence. In the end, federal officers, headed by Eliot Ness, succeeded in convicting him of not having paid enough income tax on the vast proceeds of his illegal activities. He was sentenced to eleven years in prison, most of it served in Alcatraz, but he was released in 1939 on health grounds and died a few years later of a venereal disease.

When the Eighteenth Amendment was passed I earnestly hoped… that it would be generally supported by public opinion and thus the day be hastened when the value to society of men with minds and bodies free from the undermining effects of alcohol would be generally realized. That this has not been the result, but rather that drinking has generally increased; that the speakeasy has replaced the saloon… that a vast army of lawbreakers has been recruited and financed on a colossal scale; that many of our best citizens… have openly and unabashed disregarded the Eighteenth Amendment; that as an inevitable result respect for the law has been greatly lessened; that crime has increased to an unprecedented degree I have slowly and reluctantly come to believe.

Part of a letter written in 1932 by John D. Rockefeller, Jr., a member of the wealthy family of industrialists

6   Why do you think many people did not see those who broke the prohibition laws as serious criminals?

7   What would have been the effect of the publication of the photograph, Source F?

War Near in Europe! Hillman's Amazing Revelations Start Today

Today
Prohibition Is Dead.
Bootleg Crime, Much Alive.
A Ride in California.
Bisons in Japan.

Herald Chicago and Examiner

NRA METROPOLITAN EDITION

WEDNESDAY, DECEMBER 6, 1933   Telephone Randolph 2121   TWO PARTS   PRICE 3 CENTS

PROHIBITION ERA ENDED!
LOOP CROWDS HAIL REPEAL

Repeal

By 1932, public and political opinion was frustrated by the failure of prohibition and the widespread disrespect for this particular law. On 5 December 1933, the 'noble experiment' came to an end when President Franklin Roosevelt signed the proclamation ending prohibition.

Americans turned increasingly against prohibition, which came to be seen as providing boundless opportunities for criminals as well as an infringement of liberty

H These women were celebrating their first legal drink after fourteen years of prohibition

8 What effect did increasing crime and violence have on people's attitude towards prohibition?

9 Why do you think the US Government ever expected prohibition to be successful?

10 Using all the evidence in this chapter, explain how the 'noble experiment' of prohibition became a complete failure.

Essay: Explain the different ways in which people reacted to the introduction of prohibition in 1920 and to its abolition in 1933.

Further research: Investigate the role and importance of Al Capone and his effect on public opinion.

4. *B*lack Americans

1920s–1940s

Segregation in Washington DC

This diagram is taken from the 1947 US Government Report *To Secure These Rights*

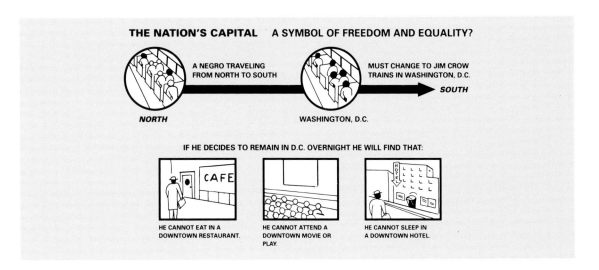

THE NATION'S CAPITAL   A SYMBOL OF FREEDOM AND EQUALITY?

A NEGRO TRAVELING FROM NORTH TO SOUTH

MUST CHANGE TO JIM CROW TRAINS IN WASHINGTON, D.C.

SOUTH

NORTH

WASHINGTON, D.C.

IF HE DECIDES TO REMAIN IN D.C. OVERNIGHT HE WILL FIND THAT:

CAFE

HE CANNOT EAT IN A DOWNTOWN RESTAURANT.

HE CANNOT ATTEND A DOWNTOWN MOVIE OR PLAY.

HE CANNOT SLEEP IN A DOWNTOWN HOTEL.

Segregation

Black population, 1920. The majority of black Americans still lived in those southern states that sixty years earlier had permitted slavery.

One group of Americans which did not share in the prosperity of the 1920s, and was even excluded, by various means, from the democratic political process, was black or African-Americans.

In 1920 about ten per cent of Americans were black and the overwhelming majority of them lived in the southern states that, sixty years earlier, had formed the slave-owning Confederacy in the Civil War. In spite of the abolition of slavery, black Americans, particularly those living in the South, endured racial discrimination and severe economic inequality.

Segregation was the cornerstone of a policy of discrimination, based solely on racial prejudice, that ensured that in the southern states blacks had the poorest standards of education; lowest paid jobs; could not eat in the same restaurants or receive treatment in the same hospitals as white people. Black and white people lived in completely separate neighbourhoods. Blacks could not expect justice from courts where the juries, lawyers and judges were always whites. Even the armed forces were segregated, out of respect for southern whites, and the Red Cross kept black people's blood segregated in blood banks until the 1940s. On buses and trains blacks had to travel in separate and always inferior facilities. Many states forbade marriage between black and white people. Washington DC, America's capital city at the northern edge of the South, was strictly segregated.

CANADA

N

MEXICO

■ Over 30% blacks

0   500   1000 km

'Jim Crow'

The laws throughout the South that enforced segregation were known as 'Jim Crow' laws, a term taken from a nineteenth-century comedian's act that ridiculed black people. In 1896 the US Supreme Court, with its *Plessey v. Ferguson* decision, gave legal approval to local state laws that segregated blacks and whites. It was an appalling decision for blacks in the South, for it legally enforced a situation that guaranteed they would never get equal status, treatment or opportunity in their own country. White southerners could protect their way of life and continue to exploit those they believed to be racially inferior, the descendants of the slaves that once upon a time had belonged to their great grandparents.

> No argument or rationalization can alter this basic fact: a law which forbids a group of American citizens to associate with other citizens in the ordinary course of daily living creates inequality by imposing a caste status on the minority group ...

These words are taken from the Report of the President's Committee on Civil Rights, *To Secure These Rights*, 1947

1. Explain the meaning of segregation?
2. Why did white Americans want segregation?
3. What was meant by 'Jim Crow' laws?

Inequality and poverty

Just as black people failed to benefit in times of prosperity, such as the 1920s, so they suffered most when times were hard. During the Great Depression (see chapter 5) black Americans bore much of the brunt of the fall in farm prices and of mass unemployment in the South. Poverty was always greater in the South than in the North, for whites as well as blacks, because the southern economy was based almost solely on agriculture, which suffered greatly from a fall in prices throughout the 1920s and 1930s. But throughout the country black Americans were always substantially worse off than were their white fellow citizens.

Educational inequality was one way of 'keeping blacks in their place' by denying them the chance to learn the skills vital for self-improvement, and also helping to ensure that ignorance made them more willing to submit to the indignities of segregation.

4. How did segregation lead to inequality?
5. How useful are Sources D and E in supporting the point of view in Source C?

Per cent of families on relief, May 1934

	Black	White
Northern cities	52.2	13.3
Border state cities	51.8	10.4
Southern cities	33.7	11.4

(Source: To Secure These Rights)

Median income of black and white families, 1935–36

City	Black	White
New York	$890	$1,930
Chicago	$726	$1,687
Atlanta*	$632	$1,876
Columbia*	$576	$1,876
Mobile*	$481	$1,419

* cities in the South

(Source: Bureau of the Census, US Department of Commerce)

Statistics of inequality

Illiteracy as a percentage of the American population

(Source: Bureau of the Census, US Department of Commerce)

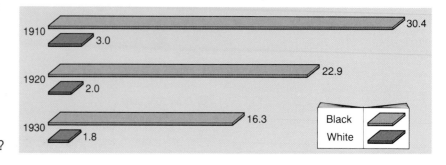

Migration to the North

Industrial expansion after the First World War created a new opportunity for black Americans, the chance to leave the South and migrate to the growing cities in the North, where, at least during periods of economic boom, they might obtain work in the factories. Between 1920 and 1930, 824,000 black people moved from the South to the North, where they could earn higher wages on a production line than they could ever expect from the mostly menial and agricultural work in the South. The North beckoned as a place free of the humiliations of segregation, and of greater economic opportunity. Nevertheless, although northern states and cities did not have legal segregation, racism was common and blacks were usually the last to be given a job, the lowest paid and the first to be fired. In the industrial cities, black neighbourhoods, known as ghettos, rapidly grew up. By 1940, 22% of blacks lived in the North, compared with only 10% in 1910.

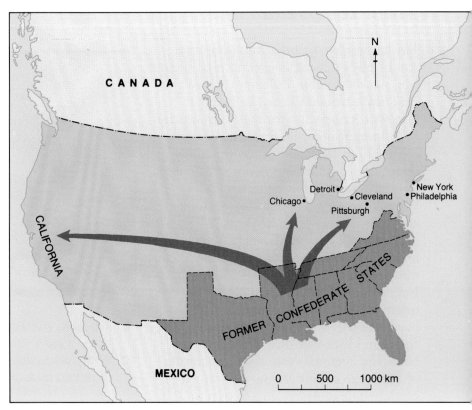

 Migration to the North. From the fields and shacks of the South, thousands of black people joined the great migration to the factories and ghettos in the North and West.

 F

...we board our first Yankee street car... we have been told that we can sit where we please, but we are still scared. We cannot shake off three hundred years of fear... A white man or a white woman comes and sits beside us, not even looking at us, as though this were a normal thing to do... Out of the corners of our eyes we try to get a glimpse of the strange white face that floats but a few inches from ours. The impulses to laugh and to cry clash in us.

An account by Young Richard Wright of the feelings of a migrant from the South travelling for the first time on a Chicago tram and experiencing life without segregation. Southerners – black and white – often use the term 'Yankee' to describe northerners.

In one district in New York, a Negro population equal in numbers to the inhabitants of Dallas, Texas, or Springfield, Massachusetts, lives works, and pursues its ideals almost as a separate entity from the great surrounding metropolis. Here Negro merchants ply their trade; Negro professional men follow their various vocations; their children are educated; the poor, sick, and orphan of the race are cared for; churches, newspapers, and banks flourish heedless of those, outside this Negro community, who resent its presence in a white city.

 G

A black writer describing Harlem in New York in the 1920s. Some historians see the great migration as a revolt; a refusal by blacks to be pushed around in the segregated South and instead to build their own communities in the North.

6 Why did so many black people leave the South?

7 In your own words, explain the feelings of Young Richard Wright in Source F.

8 How would life in Harlem, described in Source G, have been different from that in a segregated town?

Back to Africa

Two important organisations sought to recruit black Americans and to raise their consciousness about the unjust way white Americans treated them. The NAACP, National Association for the Advancement of Colored People, claimed a membership of 91,000 in 1919 and concentrated on opposing racism and segregation by means of legal action; public enquiries and various other legal and non-violent activities.

Poor black Americans, increasingly angry and frustrated, were drawn in huge numbers to Marcus Garvey's Universal Negro Improvement Association. Garvey, originally from Jamaica, argued that blacks all over the world were one people and that Africa was their homeland that had to be liberated from the colonial rule of European countries. Garvey wanted black people in America to 'return to Africa', and in 1924 he sent a deputation to Liberia to prepare the way for a settlement. But his greatest appeal lay in his assertion of pride in being black, with the slogan 'Black is beautiful'. Black, he said, was the colour of strength and beauty and not a sign of inferiority. Garvey was a brilliant and charismatic leader who thrilled people with his ideas and by impressive parades led by his African Legion in red and blue uniforms. Strong opposition to Garvey came not only from the US Government but also from moderate organisations such as the NAACP. To the great disappointment of his supporters, his grandiose ideas came to nothing and he was arrested and imprisoned for fraud. In December 1927, still maintaining his innocence, he was deported to Jamaica and later, in 1940, he died in London. In spite of the failure of Garvey's schemes, he inspired a new black consciousness and his ideas of black pride became a strong influence on the religious movement of Rastafarianism.

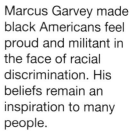

Marcus Garvey made black Americans feel proud and militant in the face of racial discrimination. His beliefs remain an inspiration to many people.

9 Why was the 'Back to Africa' movement so popular?
10 Why do you think Marcus Garvey is regarded as a great black hero?

The Ku Klux Klan

The dark side of life in America was demonstrated by the Ku Klux Klan. The Klan had been founded as a terrorist organisation of southerners, immediately after the Civil War, determined to prevent the newly freed slaves from gaining equal rights with other Americans. In the 1920s there was a resurgence of the Klan, whose members wore white masks and cloaks and used violence and terror to intimidate any American, black or white, who advocated a policy of equal rights. Only a 'WASP', white Anglo-Saxon Protestant, was eligible for membership, and the Klan was not only hostile to blacks but also to Catholics, Jews, and immigrants as well. Most Klansmen supported the upsurge of religious fundamentalism (see chapter 2). By 1925 the Klan had five million members, including police officers, judges and politicians, and was a powerful influence in several states.

On 8 August 1925 50,000 Klan members marched in Washington as a show of strength in support of white supremacy. *The Baltimore Afro-American* described the march as the greatest demonstration of intolerance ever held in a land dedicated to tolerance.

Lynchings

The most brutal treatment of black Americans was the frequent lynchings that occurred, particularly in the southern states. In many cases the local police failed to protect the victim and sometimes even played a part in the killing. Those responsible were rarely brought to justice and Klan members in particular knew that their 'friends' in the courts would not convict them. Many of the victims were probably innocent of any crime but may have been thought of as black troublemakers. In fact the real purpose of lynchings was to remind blacks forcibly that the whites were firmly in control.

Lynchings of black Americans, 1919–1941
(Source: Tuskegee Institute, Alabama)

1919	76	1928	10	1937	8
1920	53	1929	7	1938	6
1921	59	1930	20	1939	2
1922	51	1931	12	1940	4
1923	29	1932	6	1941	4
1924	16	1933	24	1952	was the
1925	17	1934	15	first year when	
1926	23	1935	18	no lynching was	
1927	16	1936	8	reported.	

When a person is lynched and the lynchers go unpunished, thousands wonder where the evil will appear again... Negroes have learned to expect other forms of violence at the hands of private citizens or public officials... Lynching is the ultimate threat by which his inferior status is driven home to the Negro... As a terrorist device, it reinforces all the other disabilities placed upon him. The threat of lynching always hangs over the head of the southern Negro; the knowledge that a misinterpreted word or action can lead to his death is a dreadful burden.

These words were also part of the report, *To Secure These Rights*, 1947

This photograph dramatically reveals the callous brutality of those white people who quite openly took part in lynchings. This scene was repeated many times and those responsible nearly always went entirely unpunished.

Why did the government fail to take action?

The Federal Government in Washington was loathe to confront the southern politicians who argued strongly for 'states rights' in opposition to federal interference and regulation. The complex relationship of state and federal laws made direct intervention against segregation or even law enforcement difficult, and national politicians feared losing white votes. Campaigning for re-election in 1924, an Indiana congressman said, 'I was told to join the Klan, or else'. They hoped that the nation's prosperity would seep down to every level and gradually eradicate inequality. In the end it was the Second World War that proved a decisive turning point for black Americans.

Chain Gang. This oil painting by William Johnson (1901-1970) shows black prisoners in a chain gang. They were a common sight in the South, where blacks were liable to serve prison sentences for quite trivial offences.

11 What were the main purposes of the Ku Klux Klan?

12 Explain what useful information an historian can learn from Source K.

13 In some parts of America the Klan and others were able to get away with terrible crimes against black people. What were these 'crimes' and why were they able to get away with them?

14 Which are the most reliable and useful sources in helping us to understand the ways in which black and white people behaved?

15 Using evidence in this chapter, explain some of the reasons why the federal government failed to stop racial discrimination.

Essay: 'The experience of black people was that they were treated in their own country as if they were not Americans at all'. Discuss this with reference to the period 1917–1947.

Further research: Examine the various ways in which black Americans opposed racism between 1917 and 1941.

5 The Great Depression

The Wall Street Crash

In spite of presidential confidence in an era of lasting prosperity, the American economy in the 1920s was not as healthy as it appeared and there were fundamental weaknesses underlying the consumer affluence. Gradually the market became glutted with goods, and prices fell as unemployment began to creep up after 1927. By the middle of 1929 the economy was already in decline, yet this was not reflected on the Wall Street stock exchange.

The value of shares had risen rapidly in what was called a 'Bull Market' as investors believed they could only profit by buying shares. People borrowed money in order to speculate in shares, and by 1929 about one million people had investments.

PRICES OF STOCKS CRASH IN HEAVY LIQUIDATION, TOTAL DROP OF BILLIONS

PAPER LOSS $4,000,000,000

2,600,000 Shares Sold in the Final Hour in Record Decline.

MANY ACCOUNTS WIPED OUT

But No Brokerage House is in Difficulties, as Margins Have Been Kept High.

ORGANIZED BACKING ABSENT

Bankers Confer on Steps to Support Market—Highest Break Is 96 Points.

The New York Times, 24 October 1929

A

Selected share prices (in Dollars)		
	3 Sept. 1929	**13 Nov. 1929**
American Can	181	86
General Electric	396	168
Montgomery Ward	137	49
	1929	**1932**
US Steel	262	22
General Motors	73	8

It appeared that the upward movement of share prices would never stop, but on 24 October, 'Black Thursday', the bottom fell out of the stock market as prices fell, and there was a stampede to sell shares before the prices fell still lower. Bankers and the government were absolutely powerless to halt the Crash, and by 29 October many of the fortunes so rapidly accumulated had been completely lost. Share prices finally hit their lowest on 8 June 1932, by which time they were lower than they had been in 1925. Millions of shares were sold for a fraction of what was paid for them.

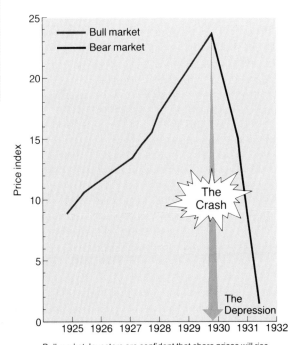

C The rise and fall of share prices, 1925–1931

Bull market: Investors are confident that share prices will rise
Bear market: Investors sell shares because the price is falling

What caused the Wall Street Crash?

Although historians cannot agree about the actual causes of the Crash, many of them think the failure to share out America's prosperity during the 1920s in an equitable manner was part of the problem.

D 'Smashup'

There was no single cause of the Crash and the ensuing Depression. but much of the responsibility for both falls on the foolhardy assumption that the special interests of business and the national interest were identical. Management had siphoned off gains in productivity in high profits, while the farmer got less, and the worker, though better off, received wage increases disproportionately small when compared to profits. As a result, the purchasing power of workers and farmers was not great enough to sustain prosperity... with no counter-action from labor unions, which were weak, or from government, which had no independent policy, business increased profits at twice the rate of the growth of productivity... profits were plunged into the stock market, producing a runaway speculation... the policies of the [Republican] federal government in the 1920s were disastrous... the [Hoover] administration took the narrow interests of business groups to be the national interest, and the result was catastrophic.

W. E. Leuchtenburg, *The Perils of Prosperity*, 1958

E

The real blame lay in the false underpinnings of the Coolidge-Hoover 'New Era' prosperity... the techniques of mass production combined to increase the efficiency per man-hour by over 40 per cent. This enormous output of goods clearly required a corresponding increase of consumer buying-power – that is higher wages. But the worker's income in the 1920s didn't rise with his productivity. In the golden year of 1929, Brookings economists calculated that to supply the barest necessities, a family would need an income of $2,000 a year – that was more than 60 per cent of American families were earning. While the rich were speculating in shares, customers of limited means were being persuaded to take products anyhow by an overextension of credit.

This is the view of American author, William Manchester in *The Glory and the Dream*, 1975

1 According to Sources D and E, what were the fundamental reasons for the fall in share prices?

Crowds gathered outside the New York Stock Exchange in Wall Street as news of the financial collapse spread. Many of these people were worried about the fate of their own investments.

Depression

The Wall Street Crash was followed by the longest and most severe Depression, from 1929 until 1941, which had repercussions in all the world's industrial nations and, as in Germany, led to serious political problems. Economic hardships, including high unemployment and poverty, affected the entire nation and led to some people seeking extreme political solutions. In Germany it was to be Nazism, whilst in America some turned to Communism and many turned to trade union agitation and protest, which was sometimes accompanied by violence.

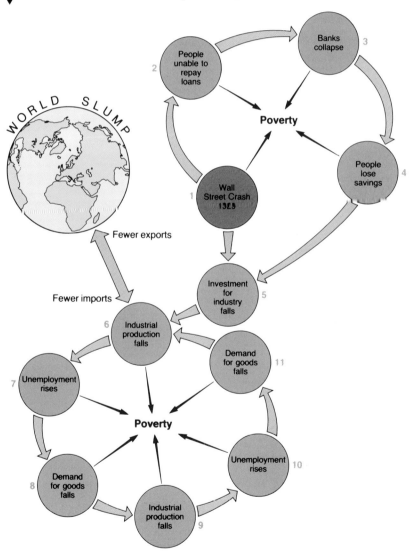

F

The USA and then the industrial world were caught in a vicious spiral of increasing unemployment and economic decline, which required the kind of radical policies which President Hoover was unwilling to adopt. The gross national product fell from $103 billion in 1929 to $55.6 billion in 1933.

G **Mass unemployment**

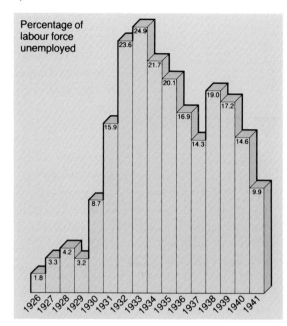

This graph shows how grim the situation was for millions of people who simply could not get a job and often had to rely on charity to survive

H **The statistics of Depression**
(Source: US Dept of Commerce)

Total Retail Sales in Stores ($000,000)

1929	1933	1937	1946
48,459	24,517	42,150	102,488

Suicides per 100,000 people

1926	12.6
1927	13.2
1928	13.5
1929	13.9
1930	15.6
1931	16.8
1932	17.4
1933	15.9
1934	14.9
1935	14.3
1936	15.0
1937	15.3
1938	14.1
1939	14.4
1940	12.8
1941	12.0

2   What were the results of the Wall Street Crash?
3   Assess the significance of the statistics in Sources G and H in helping to explain the effects of the Depression.

What was the link between the Wall Street Crash and the subsequent Great Depression?

 I

Although it did not cause the Great Depression, the collapse of the Great Bull Market did trigger it. Consumption dropped. Businesses retrenched. Marginal enterprises in farming, banking, and business went bankrupt. During the first three years after the Crash, the economy, like a tin can in a vice, was relentlessly squeezed to half its size.

Bailyn, Dallek et al, *The Great Republic*, 1992

 J

...what about the speculative boom in the stock market and the Great Crash of October 1929? Surely that episode must demonstrate the excesses of the 1920s, and the Crash must have caused or at least triggered the Depression. In fact one cannot clearly support either popular view... the Crash certainly did not start the Depression because the economy turned down in June, well ahead of the market peak.

George Green, in *Franklin Roosevelt His Life and Times*, eds O. Graham and M. Wander, 1985

4   Explain the differences in the views expressed in Sources I and J.

Bank failures

As depositors, worried that their savings were in jeopardy, tried to withdraw their money, hundreds of banks closed down altogether.

One dreadfully serious consequence of the Depression was the collapse of many banks and the loss of millions of dollars by their depositors. Many of those who had been thrifty and saved their money instead of speculating, now lost their entire savings. By the end of 1932, twenty per cent of the banks that had been operating in 1929 had closed down. People's confidence in the entire financial system was badly shaken.

 K

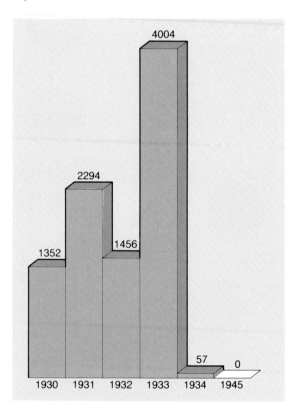

A large number of banks collapsed after the Wall Street Crash, until the 1933 *Banking Act* restored confidence

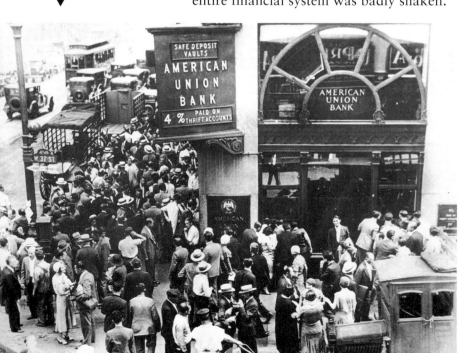

Agricultural Depression

Farmers and all those employed in agriculture were already suffering hardship before the Depression caused a further massive fall in food prices. A combination of decreased production – because Depression hit Americans were buying less – and falling food prices, cut total farm income by a half between 1929 and 1932. This in turn caused the collapse of industries and businesses that served the farming communities. Thousands of farmers lost their livelihoods and set off across America towards California seeking work. The migrants from Oklahoma and Arkansas were known as 'Okies' and 'Arkies' and their plight was immortalised by John Steinbeck in his novel *The Grapes of Wrath*. At the very depth of the Depression, farmers were hit by a disastrous drought that lasted in varying degrees for the entire 1930s. This dry spell sparked off a terrible ecological catastrophe, as the topsoil exposed after farmers removed the grasslands to enable them to plant crops, was swept up in massive dust storms that destroyed crops on a huge scale, ruined land, buried homes, and even suffocated children.

	Farm income, 1926–1933 ($000,000)	Farm wage rates per day
1926	13,302	$2.40
1929	13,938	$2.30
1933	7,107	$1.15

5   Explain how the information in Sources L and M can be used as evidence of the Depression in agriculture?

6   To what extent did natural and man-made features combine to cause hardship to those in agriculture?

 Kansas

You might truthfully say there is nothing left of western Kansas. There was not a tree, or blade of grass, or a dog or a cow, or a human being – nothing whatever, nothing at all but grey raw earth and a few farm houses and barns, sticking up from the dark grey sea like white cattle skeletons on the desert. There was nobody in the houses. The humans had given up, and gone. It was death, if I have ever seen death.

These words were written by Ernie Pyle, a well known reporter for the *Washington Daily News*, who travelled throughout America in the 1930s describing to his readers the effects of the Depression in different parts of the nation

Dust storms, as much as five miles high, in the Midwest during the 1930s wreaked havoc in areas dependent on agriculture. 150,000 square miles of farmland were destroyed. One storm alone, on 11 May 1934, blew away an estimated 300 million tons of topsoil.

Hardship and 'Hoovervilles'

From the start, President Hoover failed to grasp the severity of the Depression. In March 1930 he said: 'All the evidence indicates that the worst effects of the Crash upon unemployment will have passed during the next 60 days'. But unemployment continued to rise and was particularly severe in some cities such as Chicago, where in 1933 unemployment reached 40%. Matters were made worse because at that time there was no national system of unemployment benefit. In Chicago, local relief organisations gave the most desperate only $2.40 a week for an adult and $1.50 for a child. A dozen eggs cost 28 cents, a loaf of bread 26 cents, a pound of bacon 22 cents. Many unemployed resorted to selling apples, depending on soup kitchens, and finally to selling their homes and possessions and settling in 'Hoovervilles'. These were shanty towns, often built on rubbish tips, where families lived in dreadful conditions and were named after the President that so many blamed for their distress. In Philadelphia one official reported that hundreds of families were 'reduced for actual subsistence to something of the status of a stray cat prowling for food'.

The Bonus Army

In 1932, 20,000 unemployed men who had served in the armed forces in the First World War converged on Washington to demand assistance. For over a month many of them camped in the centre of the city not far from the presidential mansion, the White House. Some of the unemployed hoped to meet the President but instead, as tensions rose, a policeman shot two men dead. Fearful of further trouble, Hoover ordered 700 soldiers to clear the unarmed ex-servicemen out and destroy their camp. Millions of Americans were shocked by the violence that was used, and particularly the death of an eleven week-old boy fatally injured by tear-gas.

7   How reliable is Source O as evidence?
8   What would have been the effect of photographs such as this on public opinion?

In July 1932 soldiers and police attacked unemployed ex-servicemen who were camping in Washington DC, as they appealed to their government for assistance in the middle of the Depression

Responsibility

How much responsibility should be put on the Republican Presidents of the 1920s? Herbert Hoover had served under Presidents Harding and Coolidge as Secretary of Commerce, responsible for business and industrial affairs. Andrew Mellon, Hoover's Secretary of the Treasury, had been in that position since 1921.

> Mellon pulled the whistle
> Hoover rang the bell
> Wall Street gave the signal
> And the country went to hell.

This post-Wall Street Crash jingle, with its railway metaphor, reflected the opinion of many as to who was to blame

Q Who killed prosperity? (1)

> In the panic, people forgot an important fact... the wealth of the land and the energy of the people were still there... In the panic many Americans lost their heads. Everybody wanted to have somebody to blame it on... the unlucky man in the White House, the Republican Herbert Hoover, had been elected President in November 1928... he had the misfortune to be inaugurated in March 1929, just in time to get the blame for the Great Stock Market Crash... But when the collapse came so unexpectedly, President Hoover did not sit still... He brought business leaders and labor leaders to the White House, where they promised to try to keep up wages and keep factories going... he actually cut his own Presidential salary by one-fifth.

Daniel Boorstin, *Landmark History of the American People*, 1987

The electorate appeared to blame Hoover, for although he had won the 1928 election with 58% of the votes, he only received 40% when he lost the 1932 election. Many years later another Republican President, Richard Nixon, said that 'Hoover had the misfortune to hold office at the wrong time'.

R Who killed prosperity? (2)

> Hoover failed lamentably... He first coldly assured the people that the Depression was an illusion which it was their patriotic duty to ignore; then, when economic collapse occurred in Europe, he angrily denounced the Depression as something un-American from which we should isolate and insulate ourselves; and finally, truculently scolded the people for blaming the Depression on his own Republican Party which had taken full credit for the preceding boom.

This was the view of Robert Shorwood, a speechwriter for the Democrat President Franklin Roosevelt, who followed Hoover, writing in 1948

7 Why were the shanty towns called 'Hoovervilles'?
8 Explain the differing views in Sources Q and R.
9 What evidence is there in sources in this chapter to support Sources P and R?
10 How reliable are Sources P, Q and R?
11 After reading this chapter, do you agree or disagree with Richard Nixon's view that Hoover 'had the misfortune to hold office at the wrong time'?
12 What effects do you think the Depression had on the confidence of the American people in their politicians and in their economy?

Essay:
i Analyse the narrative account and the sources to explain the causes and effects of the Great Depression.
ii Why did Hoover win the 1928 election but lose in 1932?

6 The New Deal

In March 1933 Franklin Roosevelt, often simply called FDR, was sworn in as President in the middle of the greatest economic chaos the nation had ever known. Roosevelt, a Democrat, came from a wealthy family in New York State. At the age of thirty-nine he had been paralysed below the waist by polio, but with great strength of character he overcame his severe disability to become President. His experience broadened his understanding for all those who suffered disability or were underprivileged, and helped to make him one of the great liberal Presidents, believing that the power of government should be used to create a fairer society. FDR's 'New Deal' philosophy was influenced by the ideas of an American socialist, Norman Thomas.

Social duty

One of these duties of the State is that of caring for those of its citizens who find themselves the victims of such adverse circumstances as makes them unable to obtain even the necessities for mere existence without the aid of others. That responsibility is recognised by every civilised nation... To these unfortunate citizens aid must be extended by government, not as a matter of charity, but as a matter of social duty.

Franklin Roosevelt said these words in August 1931, fifteen months before the presidential election. His view of the responsibility and purpose of government was very different from that of Herbert Hoover, who was President at that time.

Roosevelt defeated Herbert Hoover by a large majority in November 1932 but had to wait four months, the 'winter of despair', before taking over as President. Shortly before taking office he survived an assassination attempt that killed the Mayor of Chicago. The gunman shouted 'Too many people are starving to death!' People had little faith in politicians and in his inaugural speech FDR had to restore confidence.

B 'Nothing to Fear'

This great nation will endure as it has endured, will revive and will prosper. So first of all let me assert my firm belief that the only thing we have to fear is fear itself – nameless, unreasoning, unjustified terror which paralyses needed efforts to convert retreat into advance... Our greatest primary task is to put people to work. it can be accomplished in part by direct recruiting by the government itself, treating the task as we would treat the emergency of a war, but at the same time, through this employment, accomplishing greatly needed projects to stimulate the use of our natural resources... I shall ask the Congress for the one remaining instrument to meet the crisis – broad executive power to wage a war against the emergency as great as the power that would be given me if we were in fact invaded by a foreign foe.

Franklin Roosevelt's inaugural speech outside the Capitol building, just after 1p.m. on 4 March 1933. The full speech lasted about 18 minutes.

> There was a bond between Roosevelt and the ordinary men and women of this country – and beyond that, between him and the ordinary men and women of the world.

Frances Perkins, a member of Roosevelt's Cabinet.

C Reactions

> It seemed to give the people, as well as myself, a new hold on life.

letter to the White House, March 1933

> I am thoroughly scared... it was full of weasel words and would let him do about what he wanted.

A Republican writing in his diary on 4 March 1933

> The President's speech had the dominant note of courageous confidence.

The Chicago Tribune, 5 March 1933.

> It is bold wisdom and action the people are praying for from President Roosevelt.

The San Francisco Chronicle, 5 March 1933

> The thing that emerges most clearly is the warning of a dictatorship.

from an article in the *New Republic*

> ROOSEVELT ASKS DICTATOR'S ROLE

Headline, *Sunday Mirror*, New York, 5 March 1933

Roosevelt promised a 'new deal for the American people' and as President he launched upon a far-reaching programme of new laws and government agencies intended to halt the Depression, create the conditions for economic growth, and give a fairer distribution of wealth. His 'New Deal' policy was a daring programme that changed the role of the federal government to an interventionist one and increased the executive power of the presidency. FDR was able to intervene in and regulate businesses and industries which before the economic crisis would have been unacceptable. A new mood of optimism encouraged businessmen to invest and to take on new employees. Nicknamed 'the Champ', FDR used his famous 'fireside chats' over the radio to win support, and he was easily re-elected in 1936, 1940 and 1944.* (* Since 1951 a President is permitted to serve a maximum of two four year terms)

Aims of the New Deal:
a Relief - measures to help the millions of unemployed
b Recovery – policies to rebuild the Depression-shattered economy
c Reform – laws to create a fairer and more just society.

1 Using Sources A and B, explain how FDR's ideas on the role of government differed from those of Coolidge and Hoover.
2 Why would FDR's views in Source A appeal to voters in 1932?
3 What were the main points Roosevelt made in his speech, Source B?
4 What was the main purpose of the speech?
5 Briefly explain the differing reactions to his speech in Source C.
6 Why did FDR use the term 'New Deal' to describe his proposals?

The Hundred Days

President Roosevelt called the US Congress into a special session, and in 100 days a whole series of measures were passed. They included:

- *Emergency Banking Relief Act* to restore confidence in the banking system
- Farm Credit Administration to assist hard hit farmers with low interest loans
- *The Home Owner's Loan Act* to provide low interest mortgages for those faced with repossession of their homes
- *The Federal Securities Act* to prevent another loss of confidence in the stock market
- Civilian Conservation Corps to provide work for men aged eighteen to twenty-five
- Federal Emergency Relief Administration to direct cash to the needy
- Tennessee Valley Authority (TVA) to revive an entire devastated region.

A large number of 'alphabet agencies', so-called because of their acronyms, were set up to push forward and supervise the New Deal policies. There was the NLB (National Labor Board), REA (Rural Electrification Administration), FSA (Farm Security Administration), and many more. The best known was the NRA (National Recovery Administration) set up in 1933. Its symbol, the blue eagle, together with the slogan 'we do our part' soon appeared on labels, newspaper mastheads, letterheads, and posters on shops and offices.

The idea was to ensure fairness in business: fair prices, fair wages and fair competition, set down in codes of fair practice. Committees of workers, employers and government officials, worked out rules and conditions that were fair for everyone in their industry. In some cases wages were raised and employment of children forbidden. Anybody unwilling to accept the NRA proposals was regarded as unpatriotic.

In early 1935, with unemployment still at around 20%, the Works Progress Administration (WPA) [renamed Works Project Administration in 1937] was set up to organise projects that would both create jobs and provide something useful at the same time. Most of them involved building, and many roads, bridges and public buildings were constructed. But WPA projects also included writing books, painting murals, looking after children and counting cattle. In 1936 more than 3,000,000 men were employed on WPA projects. Roosevelt's critics liked to complain that WPA workers spent their time 'leaning on a shovel' whilst being paid out of public funds.

▼ D FDR's plan for the WPA

The WPA should preserve not only the bodies of the unemployed from destruction, but also their self-respect, their self-confidence, and courage and determination... the projects should be useful... of a nature that a considerable portion of the money spent would go into wages... to give employment to those on the relief rolls.

President Roosevelt used these words to persuade Congress to agree to the WPA in 1935

The spirit of the New Deal, with everybody working together to aid recovery

These WPA workers who would otherwise have been unemployed are widening the street. When they spent their wages, it helped to boost demand and jobs in other industries.

▼

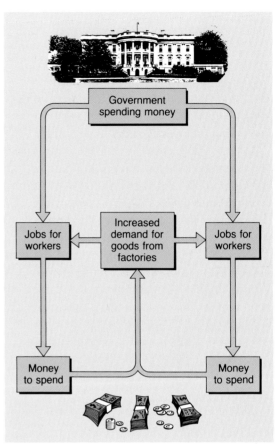

FDR's increased government spending helped to boost jobs

E Unemployment figures, 1933–1942

Year	Unemployed (millions)	% of workforce	Federal govt. employees (millions)
1933	12.8	24.9	4.3
1934	11.3	21.7	1.1
1935	10.6	20.1	4.0
1936	9.0	16.9	3.8
1937	7.7	14.3	2.7
1938	10.4	19.0	4.3
1939	9.5	17.2	3.3
1940	8.1	14.6	2.9
1941	5.6	9.9	1.8
1942	2.6	4.7	0.4

Note: The USA entered the Second World War in December 1941.

Social Security

The Great Depression had a devastating effect on the elderly. Against considerable opposition from conservative Republicans, President Roosevelt persuaded Congress to pass the 1935 *Social Security Act*. It was a considerable innovation that, for the first time, set up a national system of pensions for the elderly, widows and the disabled, paid for by a tax on workers' wages and an equivalent amount paid by employers. The Act was based on similar principles to the British old age pension scheme set up in 1909 and was one of FDR's lasting achievements.

7 Explain the purpose of the NRA.

8 Why was the WPA criticised?

9 How can Sources D and E be used to prove that the WPA was successful?

10 a By how many millions was unemployment reduced between 1933–41?

    b Is there anything in Source E that suggests a reason for the fall between 1933–1937?

11 Why was the *Social Security Act* so important?

Women in the New Deal

The New Deal saw an improvement in the status and opportunities for women because for the very first time women were taken seriously in public life. President Roosevelt appointed women to many important government posts, including Frances Perkins as Secretary of Labor, the first woman ever to serve in the US Cabinet. (The first woman Cabinet member in Britain was Labour's Margaret Bondfield in 1929.) This was at a time when most men distrusted or simply ignored women in political life. Frances Perkins had been a suffragette and she was a social reformer with a strong commitment to getting new laws passed that would benefit America's ordinary working people. She helped to prepare the important 1935 *Social Security Act* and also to draft parts of the National Recovery Administration (NRA) regulations.

Discrimination against women in employment had worsened during the Depression. Many people thought that married women were taking away jobs from unemployed men with families to support. During the 1930s most cities forbade the employment of married women as teachers, and some companies fired all their married women employees. In all industries women were paid much less than men, for example in the textile industry in 1937 the average annual income of a woman was $525 against $1,027 for a man.

Many of President Roosevelt's initiatives to tackle unemployment or provide assistance to the poor actually discriminated against women. The NRA permitted women to be paid less than men, even in the same jobs, and the *Social Security Act* gave no protection for the millions of women in domestic work. But by appointing women, President Roosevelt ensured that there were role models who would give confidence to young women to challenge barriers of discrimination. The most important woman in this respect was the President's wife, Eleanor. Their relationship was a great political partnership. She had strong opinions and used her position as First Lady to campaign against segregation and in support of New Deal reforms, often urging her husband to adopt even more liberal policies. Eleanor was constantly on the move, travelling all over the country to listen to ordinary people and to show her support for a range of liberal causes. She was extremely popular among working class and black Americans but unpopular with conservative Republicans and southern whites.

… important to women's success was the fortuitous election of Franklin Roosevelt to the presidency, for along with Franklin came Eleanor, one of the greatest two-for-one deals in American political history. Eleanor was a true friend to women in Washington. She gave women administrators free publicity at her press conferences, offered them the White House for their meetings, and most important, gave them access to the President.

F

'Two-for-one'

Susan Warr of Harvard University, writing in 1985

G

'Giving Her a Lift to Town'

Knott, *Dallas Morning News*, 22 November 1933

12 Why was the appointment of Frances Perkins significant?

13 Explain the meaning of the cartoon in Source G.

14 Why were some women disappointed by the New Deal?

15 Using each of the Sources F, and G, explain the significance of Eleanor Roosevelt.

Opposition

Critics accused FDR of seeking a 'dictatorship' or, since he came from a wealthy and distinguished family, of being a 'traitor to his class'. Southerners in his own party championed 'states rights', arguing against FDR's use of the government to interfere in areas they thought should remain with local state government. One of them, the populist Huey Long who nursed presidential ambitions himself, declared that NRA stood for 'Nuts Run America'. Long was assassinated in 1935. The American Liberty League raised huge sums of money, mostly from industrialists, to campaign against what they regarded as Roosevelt's attack on private enterprise. But the organised political opposition came from the Republican Party.

 1936 Election result

Roosevelt (*Democrat*)	**27,751,597**	(61%)
Landon (*Republican*)	**16,679,583**	(37%)

In only two out of the forty-eight states did the Republicans win more votes than FDR

More serious for Roosevelt was the opposition to some of his measures from the Supreme Court, who ruled that a number of his actions, including the NRA, were unconstitutional. However, a rapid sequence of deaths and retirements enabled him to appoint several justices who were sympathetic to the New Deal.

H 'Peril'

America is in peril... For three long years the New Deal administration has dishonoured American traditions and flagrantly betrayed the pledges upon which the Democratic Party sought and received public support... The rights and liberties of American citizens have been violated... Regulated monopoly has displaced free enterprise... It has created a vast multitude of new offices, filled them with its favorites, set up a centralised bureaucracy and sent out swarms of inspectors to harass our people... It has bred fear and hesitation in commerce and industry thus prolonging the depression... It has coerced and intimidated voters by withholding relief to those operating its tyrannical policies. It has destroyed the morale of many of our people and made them dependent upon government.

These words were the introduction to the Republican Party Platform (manifesto) for the 1936 election

"Mother Wilfred wrote a bad word!"

J Roosevelt's opponents didn't simply dislike his policies but often felt a deep personal hatred for the President himself. But efforts to discredit him failed and he won four elections.

Conclusions on Roosevelt and the New Deal

Was the New Deal successful? Roosevelt failed to reduce unemployment below ten million until the outbreak of war in Europe brought extra work to American factories. But unemployment was far lower by 1939 than it had been in 1932, and America survived the Depression without the threat of dictatorship which affected millions of people in Europe. Blacks and women failed to gain equal opportunities or a fair share of the nation's wealth. Although FDR did appoint some blacks to important government jobs, he took no stand against segregation, even though Eleanor did. He was convinced that 'hasten slowly' was the best approach towards racial equality. On the other hand, Roosevelt extended government welfare that helped all groups. He worked with the trade unions, and the ordinary working man gained greater protection and increased wages. Social security, subsidies to farmers and most of all the idea that government could and should seek to assist people in times of hardship are an enduring legacy for America from the New Deal. One journalist, Joseph Alsop, writing in 1989, described FDR's greatest achievement as 'the inclusion of the excluded'. A 1982 survey of 49 American historians ranked Roosevelt as the second greatest President out of thirty-eight – Abraham Lincoln was in first place.

 FDR and Eleanor in 1941

16 Suggest reasons why, despite the criticisms, Roosevelt had such an easy victory in the 1936 election.

17 What is the point being made by the cartoonist in Source J? Do you think cartoons such as this are an effective way to express political views?

18 What do the terms 'inclusion of the excluded' and 'forgotten man' (Source K) mean?

19 Eleanor Roosevelt wrote her memoirs, *This I Remember*. How useful do you think it would be in assisting us to know more about the life and importance of FDR?

20 How can the sources in this chapter be used to provide evidence that the New Deal was successful?

Essay:

i Explain the reactions of people to Roosevelt's New Deal policies 1933–41.

ii Which section of the community was opposed to the New Deal and what were their arguments against it?

Further research: Find out about the life of Eleanor Roosevelt and her work for the United Nations and human rights.

"Yes, You Remembered Me"

 'Yes, You Remembered Me'

Whatever the critics said, many ordinary people were grateful to FDR for the action and new laws that had improved their lives. It should be remembered that he succeeded in winning four presidential elections.

7 *F*rom isolation to war

War clouds

Preoccupied as they were with the problems of the Depression, most Americans in the 1930s were almost unaware of the growing threat to peace posed by the dictatorships in Nazi Germany and Fascist Italy, as well as Japan in the Far East. America was determined to stick to the policy of isolationism, established at the end of the First World War, and not become involved in any international disputes or wars.

What was isolationism?

Isolationists were confident that America was sufficiently protected from potential enemies by the Atlantic and Pacific Oceans. They believed that international problems were caused by others and they were not prepared to jeopardise American lives by the risk of war. The government, they argued, should concentrate on tackling America's economic problems. To back up the policy of isolationism, the US Congress passed a series of *Neutrality Acts* that were specifically intended to keep the USA out of any war.

President Roosevelt loathed the Fascist dictators, Hitler and Mussolini, but his priority was the New Deal and he was not prepared to risk it by going against public and political opinion, which was strongly isolationist. So the President said and did very little publicly about the growing international crisis. The British Prime Minister in the late 1930s, Neville Chamberlain, took the view: 'It is always best and safest to count on nothing from the Americans but words'.

1 What evidence is there in Source A that the writer is critical of Europe?
2 How does Source B disagree with Source A?
3 What was the purpose behind the Neutrality Laws?

A Death march

There can be no objection to any hand our Government may take which strives to bring peace to the world, so long as that hand does not tie 130,000,000 people into another world death march. I very much fear that we are once again being caused to feel that the call is upon America to police a world that chooses to follow insane leaders. Once again we are baited to thrill to a call to save the world.

We reach now a condition on all fours with that prevailing just before our plunge into the European war in 1917. Will we blindly repeat that futile venture?

Senator Gerald Nye, a leading supporter of Isolationism, in a 1937 newspaper article

B

Wake up! Wake up, Uncle!

This newspaper cartoon shows America, in the form of a Gulliver-like Uncle Sam, bound by pygmies representing all those intent on keeping America out of the war

War in Europe

On 1 September 1939 the German army invaded Poland in an act of unprovoked aggression. On 3 September Britain and France, acting in support of Poland, declared war on Nazi Germany. Hitler's actions shocked the American public even though a majority continued to support a policy of neutrality.

FDR was keen to do what he could to assist France and Britain, without being drawn into the war, and at the end of September it was agreed they could buy arms on a cash and carry basis. For some this was too much and the America First Committee was set up to prevent entry into the war. They opposed other organisations, including 'Bundles for Britain', set up to win support for the Allies.

▼ F What the people think, September 1939

Enter the war on the side of England, France, and Poland	2.5%
Support Germany	0.2%
Keep out of the war but sell to anyone on a cash and carry basis	37.5%
Keep out of the war but sell to England, France and Poland, but not Germany	8.9%
Keep out of the war but go in on the side of England and France if they are in danger of losing	14.7%
Have nothing to do with any warring country – no trade	29.9%
Other views including don't know	6.3%
	_____
	100%

This opinion poll was carried out just after the start of the war and was certainly read by President Roosevelt. Many of those who wanted trade with at least some of the warring countries saw it as an opportunity to help American business and reduce unemployment.

▼ G US must keep out of Europe's war

We can keep out of war if we want to.
Europe could keep out of war if it wanted to.
There is no situation in Europe which could not have been solved by the peaceful discussion which the President urged.
But the traditional hatreds and jealousies and the long established warlike habits of Europe made war inevitable there.
But war is in no sense inevitable here.

This comment, by the newspaper tycoon William Randolph Hearst, was published on the front page of many of America's newspapers on the day after Britain and France declared war on Germany

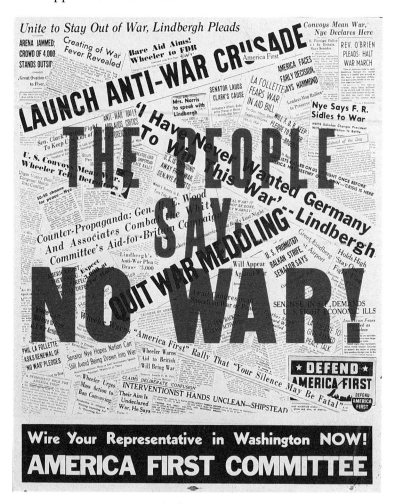

 In 1940 many Americans either felt that Britain and France were doomed or that the war in Europe posed no threat to the USA. Isolationists included a disparate group of politicians, Republican and Democrat, who were usually opposed to one another.

With the defeat of France in June 1940, it was clear that even if Britain survived, she would not be able to liberate those tragic nations occupied by the German army. The war against Hitler could only be won if Russia and America joined in against him. But President Roosevelt, campaigning for re-election to a third term as President, continued to reassure voters that the USA would not enter the war.

◤H◥ 'Your boys'

> And while I am talking to you mothers and fathers, I give you one more assurance. I have said this before, but I shall say it again and again and again: Your boys are not going to be sent into any foreign wars.

FDR made this comment in a famous campaign speech in Boston just a few days before he won re-election in 1940

Once re-elected, Roosevelt moved quickly to give greater assistance to beleaguered Britain. America was going to be the 'arsenal of democracy' and he openly warned that if Germany were to overrun Britain and destroy the Royal Navy, then the USA would be vulnerable.

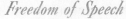

OURS...to fight for

Freedom of Speech *Freedom of Worship*

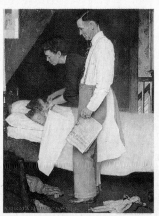

Freedom from Want *Freedom from Fear*

> The first phase of the invasion of this hemisphere would not be the landing of regular troops, the necessary strategic points would be occupied by secret agents and their dupes – and great numbers of them are already here and in Latin America.
> ... Let us say to the democracies: We Americans are vitally concerned in your defence of freedom... We shall send you, in ever-increasing numbers, ships, planes, tanks, guns. This is our purpose and our pledge... we will not be intimidated by the threats of dictators ...
> ... we look forward to a world founded upon four essential freedoms.
> The first is freedom of speech and expression – everywhere in the world.
> The second is the freedom of every person to worship God in his own way – everywhere in the world.
> The third is freedom from want... everywhere in the world.
> The fourth is freedom from fear... everywhere in the world.

This poster 'The Four Freedoms' by Norman Rockwell (1894-1978) gave a powerful visual expression to FDR's explanation of the principles that Americans stood for. In 1943 more than four million of these posters were printed and helped establish Rockwell as the most famous American artist in the 20th Century. But although Rockwell is enormously popular for portraying the ideals of the American Dream, yet he remains treated with disdain by most of the art establishment.

◀I The four freedoms

This speech by President Roosevelt, on 6 January 1941, set out clearly the things that he believed most of the American people were prepared to fight for. Isolationists saw it as a clear indication that FDR planned to take America into the war.

The Lend-Lease scheme in early 1941 was to supply military and other goods to any nation whose defence the President considered vital to the USA. A secret meeting between Roosevelt and the British Prime Minister, Winston Churchill, in August 1941 cemented the relationship between the two nations with a set of common principles in the Atlantic Charter. The inclusion of a call for the 'final destruction of the Nazi tyranny' was astonishing while the USA was still supposedly neutral. Roosevelt stepped up naval patrols in the Atlantic Ocean and protected British convoys as far as Iceland. When a German submarine fired a torpedo at a US ship that was actually stalking it, Roosevelt ordered the Navy 'to shoot on sight'. Some historians believe he was deliberately trying to provoke Hitler into sinking American ships so that he could overcome isolationist opposition and get Congress to declare war on Germany.

5 What evidence is there in Source G that the writer is critical of Europe?
6 Who would have drawn the most comfort from Source G, the isolationists or supporters of Britain and France?
7 How do sources F and G help us understand Roosevelt's words in Source H?
8 Why do you think Roosevelt talked about the 'four freedoms'?
9 Why were isolationists concerned over FDR's actions and statements during 1941?
10 Describe the ways in which the USA assisted Britain during 1940-41.
11 What do you think Germany's attitude towards American 'neutrality' would have been?

Pearl Harbor

But, almost unexpectedly, war came not from Germany but from the Far East, with a massive surprise attack by Japan on the US base at Pearl Harbor in Hawaii. Hardly anyone, even government experts, had thought that Japan would dare to mount such an attack on the USA.

Throughout the 1930s, America had been increasingly concerned over Japan's growing power in the Far East. When Japan took over French Indo-China during 1941, Roosevelt froze all Japanese money and assets in the USA. Relations between the two countries steadily deteriorated and the Japanese began preparing for war. Although US intelligence had broken Japan's secret code, and knew of these preparations, they still could not believe Japan would actually attack and certainly not in Hawaii.

At dawn on Sunday 7 December 1941, waves of Japanese planes bombed a completely unprepared American fleet at anchor. The losses were dreadful, including 177 planes, five battleships, and five other vessels lost, and there was serious damage to a further eight vessels. Casualties were 2343 killed and 1272 wounded. To the Japanese it was a brilliant victory that had knocked out the American Pacific Fleet at the very start of the war. To the Americans it was an act of murderous treachery, carried out before war had been declared. President Roosevelt called it 'a day of infamy' and the next day Congress formally declared war on Japan. Britain immediately joined the USA against Japan. On 11 December Germany, who had a pact with Japan, declared war on the USA. Another consequence was that the USA was now allied with the Communist Soviet Union, who had been attacked by Hitler in June 1941. Most American doubts and the isolationists were silenced by the Japanese attack. Pearl Harbor united the country behind the President as America mobilised for total war.

Reactions

J Remember Dec. 7th

...we here highly resolve that these dead shall not have died in vain...

REMEMBER DEC. 7th!

K 'Hail Columbia'

Punch cartoon 1942

L Winston Churchill

So we had won after all!... We had won the war. England would live; the Commonwealth of Nations and the Empire would live... We should not be wiped out. Our history would not come to an end. We might not even have to die as individuals. Hitler's fate was sealed. Mussolini's fate was sealed. As for the Japanese they would be ground to powder.

These were Winston Churchill's feelings after Pearl Harbor had brought America into the war on the side of Britain

M President Roosevelt

We may acknowledge that our enemies have performed a brilliant feat of deception, perfectly timed and executed with great skill. It was a thoroughly dishonourable deed... We don't like it — we didn't want to get in it — but we are in it, and we're going to fight it with everything we've got.

Roosevelt speaking on the radio on 9 December 1941

12 How do you think these people would have reacted to the news of the Japanese attack on Pearl Harbor?
a President Roosevelt
b isolationists
c supporters of Britain
d young men
e young women.
13 What was the purpose of the poster, Source J?
14 What view does the cartoon, Source K, take of America's entry into the war?
15 Explain the reasons for Churchill's view in Source L.
16 Why did American opinion over involvement in the war change between 1939 and 1941?

Essay: Describe the policy of President Roosevelt from the start of the Second World War until the entry of the USA in December 1941.

Further research: Examine the way in which the Japanese prepared and carried out the attack on Pearl Harbor.

8 America at war
1941–45

Key events for Americans

1941

7 December	Japan attacks Pearl Harbor
8 December	USA declares war on Japan
11 December	Germany and Italy declare war on USA

1942

127,000 Japanese-Americans forcibly moved to detention centres

4–7 June	First Japanese defeat at Battle of Midway
8 November	America and Britain invade Algeria

1943

May	War contractors barred from racial discrimination
9 September	American troops invade Italy

1944

6 June	American and Allied forces invade France on D-Day
7 November	Roosevelt re-elected to a third term

1945

February	Roosevelt meets with Stalin and Churchill at Yalta
19 February	US Marines land at Iwo Jima
1 April	America invades Okinawa
12 April	Roosevelt dies of a cerebral haemorrhage and Harry Truman becomes President
7 May	Germany surrenders
6 August	America drops atomic bomb on Hiroshima
9 August	America drops atomic bomb on Nagasaki
15 August	Japan surrenders

The massive American commitment of fighting men as well as of resources proved to be a decisive factor in achieving allied victory over Germany and Japan. The government took on additional powers to direct the war effort, both by the conscription of men for the armed forces, and through the direction of the economy, by instructing companies what they should produce in their factories. With around 12 million people serving in the army, navy or air force, it was America's biggest ever military mobilisation. This large-scale conscription into the armed forces brought about many changes which affected women and black Americans in particular.

▲ President Roosevelt signing the declaration of war

▼ Strength in numbers. US active duty forces in millions 1900-1985.

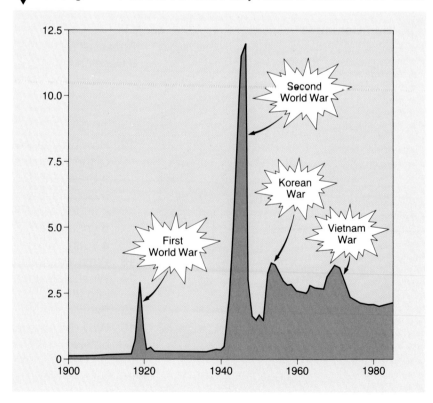

The impact of the war

The Second World War brought an end to the Depression in the United States and created an economic boom that has never been equalled. New businesses sprang up whilst old ones suddenly had full order books and could take on new workers. The war economy, coupled with good weather in the years 1941–45, boosted agriculture, as farmers had a guaranteed market in feeding the armed forces. Those Americans who did not have to leave their homes to go and fight, enjoyed a rapid increase in their income and their standard of living. Because there was no fighting or air raids on the American mainland, most civilians, unlike in Europe and Asia, had no direct experience of the war.

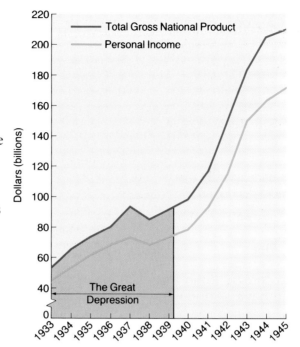

Recovery of the US economy

What was the War like?

 The GI*

> Maybe he huddled at night in a hole dug in jagged coral or clammy sand and prayed. 'God, let me get hit tomorrow but not bad, so I can get out of this'. Maybe he didn't fight at all. Maybe he built latrines in Mississippi or cranked a mimeograph machine in Manila... still wanting to go home.
> He was often bored; he wasn't always brave; many times he was scared.
> Maybe he was young, or maybe he wasn't so young, like Jack Privett, a 37 year old pfc, who was killed in the Battle of Luxembourg and left a wife and five kids back in Blytheville, Arkansas.
> Maybe he's just a memory in a photo album now, or a dogtag stuck on a cross of wood near a tiny town whose name you can't pronounce.'

These words by Sgt. Debs Myers appeared in the soldier's own magazine YANK in 1945.

* The term GI meant 'government issue' and was stamped on every piece of a soldier's equipment, and soon came to mean even the soldier himself.

D 'Relative comfort'

We live in the light*, in relative comfort and complete security. We are the only nation in this war which has raised its standard of living since the war began. We are not tired, as all Europe is tired.

Broadcaster Ed Murrow speaking on CBS radio during the war

* There was no real blackout in America

E The woman on the bus

During March 1942, according to an anecdote, a woman on a bus was reported to have said loudly, 'Well, my husband has a better job than he ever had and he's making more money, so I hope the war lasts a long time'. At that, another woman rose and slapped her face, blurting out, 'That's for my boy who was killed at Pearl Harbor, and this' – a second slap – 'is for my boy on Bataan'.

A story told by the writer William Manchester in *The Glory and the Dream*, 1974. (The Japanese defeated the Americans in April 1942 on the Islands of Bataan after three months of fighting.)

F Corregidor

Corregidor here Corregidor here 0200 5 May 42 They are not here yet We are waiting for God only knows what How about a chocolate soda Lots of heavy fighting going on We may have to give up by noon They bring in the wounded every minute The jig is up Everyone is bawling like a baby They are piling dead and wounded in our tunnel I know how a mouse feels Caught in a trap waiting for guys to come along and finish it up My name is Irving Strobing Get this to my mother Mrs Minnie Strobing 605 Barbey Street Brooklyn New York.

One of the last radio messages received from US troops trapped by the Japanese on the island of Corregidor just before their capture in May 1942

Production for war

America has almost unlimited natural resources of raw materials. There were shortages of some goods in US stores but it led to only a little inconvenience. Factories that had been churning out domestic products such as cars and typewriters were directed by the War Production Board (WPB) to the production of arms and equipment for all the allied forces. The Office of Scientific Research and Development mobilised thousands of scientists to develop new methods of death from bazookas to the atomic bomb, as well as new methods of saving the lives of those wounded in battle. The cost of the war to the government was vast. Government expenditure rose from $20 billion in 1941 to $97.2 billion in 1944. Taxes were increased, people were persuaded to save money in the form of war bonds, and the national debt grew to six times the size it was in 1941. Most of this money went to the largest corporations because only they had the factories suitable for producing ships, aircraft and tanks.

A US Army Air Force Poster

G War Production, 1941–1945

Warplanes	296,429
Tanks	102,351
Artillery pieces	372,431
Trucks	2,445,964
Aircraft bombs	5,822,000
Small guns	20,086,061
Ammunition for small guns	44,000,000,000 (rounds)

1 According to Source A, what effect did the war have on the economy?
2 Which sources, A–F, are the most reliable?
3 Why was the second woman in Source E angry?
4 Is there any information in Sources A–D and F which helps us to understand the two women in Source E?
5 What do the Sources B-F tell us about the differing experience of Americans in the war?

Women at war

The war years increased opportunities for women and permanently improved their status. Six million women entered factories engaged in war production and learned and used skills that previously had been male occupations. Nearly two hundred thousand joined the armed forces in the Women's Army Corps (WACs), or the Navy's Women Accepted for Volunteer Emergency Service (WAVES). Still more joined the American Red Cross and served overseas, bringing comfort and care to the troops. Some lost their lives.

Working in a factory often brought higher wages than the jobs the women had previously done. Women worked as machinists, toolmakers, stevedores and railroad track layers. Sales of women's trousers during 1942 were five times what they had been in 1941, because of factory work. As men left their jobs to join the forces, so women took the opportunity to prove that any job could be equally well performed by a woman, and some were unwilling to concede that important principle once the war was over.

H Production

This 1942 poster issued by the Office for Emergency Management uses graphic design techniques perfected in commercial advertising to motivate civilian war production workers

I She's a WOW

The woman behind the man. This poster encouraging women to work in a factory perhaps contains a hint that it is only for the duration of the war.

Rosie the Riveter

Posters such as these presented a new image of women and a new role model for them. Rosie the Riveter became a powerful symbol of women taking over traditionally men's work.

Many women were keen to get away from domestic chores, particularly if their husband was away in the forces. Child-minding services and for the first time factory nurseries were set up so that mothers could work. In 1940 about 35% of married women worked, but that increased to 50% by 1945. By the summer of 1944, over a third of all workers were women, which was a quite unprecedented figure. Some fathers or husbands complained about this trend, but women could justifiably claim it was a patriotic duty that took them from the home to work in a shipyard or aircraft factory.

It was the first time I had a chance to get out of the kitchen and work in industry and make a few bucks. This was something I had never dreamed would happen.

These were the feelings of a woman who had a wartime job as a welder

But although many women moved from low paying jobs or, in the case of housewives, no pay at all to higher paid factory work, equal work did not mean equal pay and women received far lower wages than men. Many male workers still retained prejudice against working women and certainly most men took the view that when the war was over they should revert to their traditional roles and the jobs be made available to the returning soldiers.

In a great many cases that happened, but traditional attitudes had been undermined and the confidence of women strengthened, so that in the long term the rights and opportunities of women were greatly extended.

Black Americans at war

How could the USA fight for freedom against the racism of Nazi Germany and yet continue to practice segregation and discrimination against black and other ethnic groups? How, it was asked, could a 'Jim Crow' army fight for a free world? For some Americans, blacks and the Japanese Americans, FDR's 'four freedoms' did not seem to apply. Even in the armed forces segregation remained. (They were not integrated until 1948.) Yet the war did bring advancement in opportunities for black Americans and created the conditions that eventually led to the end of segregation. A comment during the war from black soldiers was, 'It'll be different after the war'.

1,154,720 blacks joined or were conscripted into the armed forces to serve in segregated units. In many cases black soldiers ended up doing the menial work in labour battalions and still suffered insults from whites, including sometimes their commanding officers. In Britain, where more than a million and a half GIs were stationed, there was frequent conflict between black and white soldiers. White GIs from the southern states were upset that British pubs, cinemas and buses, did not operate any racial segregation.

L **American racism in Britain**

I have personally seen the American troops kick, and I mean kick, coloured soldiers off the pavements, and when asked why, reply 'stinking black pigs' or 'black trash' or 'uppity niggers'.

This wartime recollection is from an Englishman in Birmingham

English people soon got used to the sight of black US soldiers with their unique style of high-step marching in the high streets of country towns

English people could not understand why the US seemed to have two entirely separate armies – one black the other white. The American tensions increased when black soldiers went out with local white girls.

The British population lacks the racial consciousness which is so strong in the United States. The small-town British girl would go to a movie or a dance with a Negro quite as readily as she would go with anyone else, a practice that our white soldiers could not understand. Brawls often resulted and our white soldiers were further bewildered when they found that the British press took a firm stand on the side of the Negro.

The view of General Dwight Eisenhower, US Commander in Chief of the Allied Forces in Western Europe in charge of the D-Day invasion of 1944. Later (1954) he was elected President.

A black GI with an English girl in July 1943. This would have been illegal in the southern USA but in Britain black soldiers experienced the freedom to mix equally with whites that they were denied in their own country.

As well as in the fighting forces, black Americans played an important part on the home front. By the end of 1944 about two million were working in war factories, and large numbers of southern blacks migrated from the segregated South to the industrial cities in the North. For these people a job in a factory or service in the army usually brought better wages than they had had before.

Service for their country, coupled with the fact that the war was being waged against the Nazis, raised the expectations of many black Americans. It had to be a war not just against Hitler but also against Hitlerism, and the 'Double V' campaign stood for victory at home and abroad. Membership of the NAACP, the main campaigning black organisation, rose from 50,000 to 450,000 during the four years of war. Pressure on the President caused him to forbid any company with a contract for war equipment to practise discrimination. This increased demand for justice provoked antagonism from bigoted whites and racial violence flared in several places.

6 What is the difference in the message of the poster in Source I and the one in Source J?
7 How did the war affect women?
8 Why was the US Army segregated?
9 What effect might being stationed in Britain have had on a black soldier?
10 What do you think was meant by the phrase, 'It'll be different after the war'?

Japanese Americans

One episode, now accepted as quite shameful, was the brutal treatment of 80,000 US citizens of Japanese origin, the Nisei, and another 47,000 Issei who were born in Japan and forbidden by law to become US citizens. 90% of them lived in the West Coast states and many of them in Los Angeles. Following the attack on Pearl Harbor, a wave of anti-Japanese prejudice was directed against these people, together with a wholly unjustified fear that they might be disloyal and assist a Japanese invasion of the West Coast. With complete disregard for their civil rights, President

Japanese Americans being forced to register as they arrived at an internment camp in 1942. They were the victims of panic and prejudice.

Roosevelt authorised their immediate forced transportation to remote and uncomfortable internment camps. Many lost their homes and businesses and it is estimated that in all they lost over $400 million worth of property and possessions. Some of them were so angry that they refused to pledge their loyalty to the USA, and more than a thousand were shipped to Japan. Nowadays it seems incredible that they could have been so mistreated and eventually in 1988 the government gave a formal apology and made some financial compensation to the 60,000 still alive.

11 German and Italian Americans were not treated in the same way as Japanese Americans. Why do you think this was?

12 Was the President right to put national security and the worries of many Americans before the civil liberties of the Nisei?

Victory

In May 1945 Hitler committed suicide and Germany unconditionally surrendered. The USA had played a major role in the invasion of Europe in June 1944 and, together with the British, Canadian and French armies, had liberated the western European countries that had endured Nazi occupation. Then they crossed the Rhine and invaded Germany itself. The Russians had entered Germany from the East and met up with the American soldiers at the River Elbe on 25 April 1945. Less than two weeks later the war in Europe had ended. President Roosevelt, exhausted and in poor health during the latter part of the war, had died suddenly on 12 April. Less than six months earlier he had easily won re-election to a fourth term of office with 56% of the votes. The nation mourned the only President that younger Americans had ever really known and who had earned such massive support, firstly for his New Deal and then for his wartime leadership.

The new President, Harry Truman, was immediately faced with the awesome decision of having to give approval for the dropping of the first atomic bomb, which had been developed in great secrecy as the Manhattan Project at the instigation of President Roosevelt in 1941. Some advisors said it should be dropped somewhere relatively harmless, as a warning to Japan. Recent research supports the view that Japan may have been willing to surrender before Truman gave the orders to drop the new bombs, firstly on the Japanese city of Hiroshima, with the loss of 80,000 lives, and then on Nagasaki with the loss of 35,000 people. The atomic age had begun, and only America possessed this new devastating weapon. Faced with this the Japanese government surrendered on 2 September 1945.

The consequences of the war

The USA was in a much stronger position at the end of the war than in 1941. American casualties had been relatively light compared with the losses of other nations, with about 400,000 Americans killed in battle, which was roughly the same number that died on America's roads during the 1940s.

The war had four main consequences for America:

- The USA had a strong economy. Only in the United States were people better off than before the war. American banks became the world's bankers. Only the USA could help the war-shattered economies of other countries.
- The USA had a new powerful role in world affairs. America's important contribution to the defeat of Germany and Japan, and her monopoly of the atomic bomb, made her a world superpower. American bases now existed all over the world and American soldiers occupied parts of Germany, Austria and Japan. The USA promoted setting up the United Nations with its headquarters in New York.

- American technology, stimulated by the needs of the war, now led the world. American companies were well ahead of any competitors and ready to expand as multi-national companies, so that American trademarks became well known around the world.
- America's role in liberating countries conquered by Hitler created enormous admiration and gratitude from their peoples. Hollywood films, popular music, and many new consumer products, made America's apparently comfortable lifestyle the envy of people in countries where there was great hardship immediately after the war.

13 Why was the USA in a stronger position than other countries, such as Britain or Russia, in 1945?

14 How did the war change America's role in world affairs?

Essay:

i Assess the impact of the war on the American people.

ii Using information from Chapters 6, 7 and 8, describe and assess the achievements of President Roosevelt.

The surrender ceremony. On 2 September 1945 the Japanese formally surrendered to General Douglas MacArthur on board the battleship USS Missouri in Tokyo Bay.

President Harry Truman

9 America and the Cold War

Shortly after the end of the Second World War, serious disagreements divided the USA and Britain from their former wartime ally, the USSR. A bitter Cold War, as it came to be known, led to conflict and confrontation with frequent disagreement at the United Nations (UN) that at times threatened to boil over into a full-blooded war. The main area of disagreement was Eastern Europe, particularly countries such as Poland, Romania and Hungary, which had been occupied by the Red Army as they drove back the Germans. Germany itself was divided into zones of occupation by the four allies and her former capital, Berlin, was also split among the allies into four zones and occupied by British, French, American and Soviet troops. The entire city, however, was contained within the Soviet zone of East Germany, and on several occasions Berlin was the focus of tension between the USSR and the West. In almost every country occupied by the Soviet Union, Communist pro-Russian governments took over. On a visit to the USA, Winston Churchill, Britain's former wartime Prime minister, declared that an 'Iron Curtain' had descended down the centre of Europe behind which Eastern European Communist governments controlled from Moscow were seeking 'to obtain totalitarian control'. The Communist system of one party government with State ownership of all industries and control of the press and radio, was wholly at odds with America's belief in private enterprise capitalism and a two party political system, and a freedom of the press guaranteed by the American Constitution.

The Truman Doctrine

In March 1947 President Truman set out a tough line for American policy towards the USSR and any attempt by them to spread Communism to other countries. He was particularly concerned at Soviet efforts to gain domination over Turkey and Greece.

Containment
▼
A

The very existence of the Greek state is today threatened by the terrorist activities of several thousand armed men, led by Communists... Greece must have assistance if it is to become a self-supporting and self-respecting democracy. The United States must supply this assistance... there is no other country to which democratic Greece can turn... as in the case of Greece, if Turkey is to have the assistance it needs, the United States must supply it. We are the only country able to provide that help ...

The peoples of a number of countries of the world have recently had totalitarian regimes forced upon them against their will... I believe that it must be the policy of the United States to support free peoples who are resisting attempted subjugation by armed minorities or by outside pressures.

I believe that we must assist free peoples to work out their own destinies in their own way.

I believe that our help should be primarily through economic and financial aid, which is essential to economic stability and orderly political process ...

The free peoples of the world look to us for support in maintaining their freedoms.

This was part of President Truman's speech to the Congress on 12 March 1947 at a time when the USSR was encouraging Communist takeovers in Greece and Turkey. Truman's policy was one of 'containment' which meant preventing any further Russian expansion of power over other nations. It soon became known as the 'Truman Doctrine'.

◄ Truman made this slogan famous by keeping the sign on his desk to remind himself, and everybody else, that he was ultimately responsible for whatever happened. Truman's domestic policies, known as the 'Fair Deal', were overshadowed by the emergence of the Cold War and the failure to gain complete victory in the Korean War.

Who was to blame for the Cold War?

The Truman Doctrine made it clear that the USA would be actively involved in the internal affairs of other countries in order to stop the spread of Communism. It was a clear declaration of hostility towards the USSR that was bound to provoke antagonism and perpetual quarrelling between the two nations. Some people claimed that it was the USA getting tough that was responsible for the 'Cold War'. Supporters of Truman argued that it was entirely the fault of the USSR by trying to impose, often by force or underhand methods, a Communist system on others. One unfortunate result of Truman's policy was that the USA sometimes, as in Greece in 1947, ended up supporting repressive or corrupt politicians simply because they were anti-Communist. The policy often appeared to be primarily anti-Soviet rather than a positive commitment to democratic government. American confidence in taking a firm line with the USSR was strengthened by their monopoly of the atomic bomb, and public opinion was firmly behind the principle of 'getting tough with Russia'.

In 1949 the USA recruited many West European countries, together with Canada, into the North Atlantic Treaty Organisation (NATO), a military alliance intended to oppose any Soviet attack across the 'Iron Curtain'. NATO was the military arm of the 'Truman Doctrine'. After West Germany joined in 1954, the USSR set up an East European equivalent, the Warsaw Pact, in 1955, to confront NATO.

1 What did Churchill mean by the term 'Iron Curtain'?
2 What reasons did Truman give (Source A) for his policy?
3 Why was Truman's policy described by the word 'containment'?
4 What reaction would you expect the USSR to have given to the 'Truman Doctrine'?
5 How did the atomic bomb influence American policy?

The Marshall Plan

The European Recovery Program (ERP), usually known as the Marshall Plan, was the practical carrying out of the Truman Doctrine, although it was not presented as that at the time. General George Marshall, a former senior army commander, served as the Secretary of State, the American equivalent of Foreign Secretary, during the years 1947–49. The Marshall Plan provided $12.5 billion to sixteen nations and reduced the likelihood of vulnerable countries choosing Communist governments. At the time it was presented as a selfless act and the British Foreign Secretary, Ernest Bevin declared, 'The generosity of it was beyond belief'. The Plan helped to rebuild war-shattered European economies, including Britain's, and ensured a politically and economically stable Western Europe able to stem the spread of Soviet influence. The Marshall Plan also firmly established the USA as the leader of the western nations, or as it was often said 'leader of the free world'. The USSR complained of American arrogance and even some non-Communists questioned America's right to interfere in the affairs of other nations. Truman and Marshall were accused of intensifying the Cold War.

Confrontation in Berlin. The USSR tested American determination by cutting all land routes to West Berlin from April 1948 to September 1949. American and British aircraft overcame the blockade by flying more than 2,000,000 tons of food and coal into the city. Berlin was the scene of numerous Cold War incidents and a constant source of tension.

FOR EUROPEAN RECOVERY
SUPPLIED BY THE
UNITED STATES OF AMERICA

B The Marshall Plan

It is logical that the United States should do whatever it is able to do to assist in the return of normal economic health in the world, without which there can be no political stability and no assured peace. Our policy is directed not against any country or doctrine but against hunger, poverty, desperation and chaos... governments, political parties or groups which seek to perpetuate human misery in order to profit therefrom, politically or otherwise, will encounter the opposition of the United States.

This was how George Marshall explained his plan for the first time in a speech on 5 June 1947 at Harvard University

D The real reasons

The appraisal was that, without massive dollar aid, the European economy would sink to a level so low that Communism would find ready recruits and all or most of continental Europe would, within a year or two, be in the greatest danger of falling into the control of the Soviet Union. There were other reasons given and other motives but this – essentially the Truman Doctrine – was the necessary and sufficient cause of the ERP...

The real reason for the Marshall Plan was admitted in this secret government report written in August 1950

C The Soviet View

This extract is from a speech by Vyshinsky, the Soviet representative at the United Nations in September 1947

It is becoming more and more evident to everyone that the implications of the Marshall Plan will mean placing European countries under the economic and political control of the United States.
Moreover, this plan is an attempt to split Europe into two camps and, with the help of Britain and France, to complete the formation of a bloc of several European countries hostile to the interests of the democratic countries of Eastern Europe and most particularly to the interests of the Soviet Union. An important feature of this plan is an attempt to create a bloc of Western European states, including Western Germany. The intention is to make use of German heavy industry as one of the most important economic bases for American expansion into Europe.

FÜR EUROPAS WIEDERAUFBAU
VEREINIGTEN STAATEN VON AMERIKA
BELGRAD
Bremen 3883

 Bags of flour being supplied to Yugoslavia under the Marshall Plan

E How Europe recovered and grew, 1947–1951
(Source: US Department of State)

Per capita income in selected Marshall Plan countries (in US dollars)

	1947	1951
Austria	891	1816
West Germany	1320	2507
Greece	505	659
Iceland	2427	2948
Italy	844	1071

These figures show the average income per person. For the average citizen in the 16 Marshall Plan countries life improved by 33% between 1947 and 1951. The Marshall Plan was hailed as a great success and because of it, in 1953, George Marshall became the only military man to ever win the Nobel Peace Prize for his contribution to world peace.

6   How reliable are Sources B to E?
7   How do Sources B, C and D, differ in their explanation of the purpose of the Marshall Plan?
8   What criticism might have been made by the Soviets of the award of the Nobel Peace Prize to George Marshall in 1953?

The Korean War

America's determination to halt any expansion of Communism received its sternest challenge when, on 25 June 1950, Soviet-backed North Korean troops invaded non-Communist South Korea. With the support of the United Nations, President Truman ordered US troops, under the command of General MacArthur, into Korea to attempt to drive the North Koreans back. Both Communist China and the USSR gave massive support to the North Koreans. It was the most serious Cold War crisis which threatened to bring all-out war with Russia and China against the USA. But American troops fought under the flag of the UN, and technically the war was described as a 'police action of the United Nations'. The US provided 48% of the troops, 43% were South Koreans, and the remaining 9% came from a total of seventeen other nations, including Britain and Australia.

◤ 'We are not at war'

We are not at war... The Republic of Korea was set up with United Nations help. It was unlawfully attacked by a bunch of bandits who are neighbors, in North Korea. The United Nations held a meeting and asked the members to go to the relief of the Korean Republic, and the members of the United Nations are going to the relief of the Korean Republic, to suppress a bandit raid on the Republic of Korea. That is all there is to it ...

President Truman speaking at a White House press conference in June 1950, to explain the difference between a war and a 'police action'. Nobody was convinced and it was always described by everybody else as the Korean War and regarded as an American-led operation.

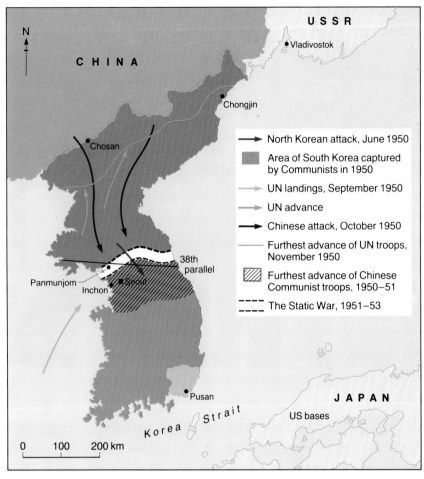

Key:

➤ North Korean attack, June 1950

■ Area of South Korea captured by Communists in 1950

➤ UN landings, September 1950

➤ UN advance

➤ Chinese attack, October 1950

— Furthest advance of UN troops, November 1950

▨ Furthest advance of Chinese Communist troops, 1950–51

---- The Static War, 1951–53

The war went badly for the USA and early enthusiasm for this actual head-on conflict with the Communists evaporated as the American-backed armies were forced to retreat. In October 1950, China sent a powerful army to support the North Koreans. Public disagreements between President Truman and General MacArthur finally ended with the general being relieved of his command. MacArthur had wanted to attack China, possibly with atomic bombs, but this was opposed by the President who, as Commander-in-Chief, could not accept his general's open disagreement. The problem for Truman was that MacArthur was enormously popular, and on his return to America he was hailed as a great hero with a parade through New York and an emotional speech to the US Congress that was broadcast on TV.

▲

North and South Korea. The proximity of the USSR worried President Truman that the Korean War could have led to a third world war between America and the USSR.

These US soldiers were taken prisoner of war in Korea. This humiliation for America in Asia was to be repeated in the 1960s in Vietnam.

Gallup opinion poll, July 1951

F

Do you think the United States made a mistake going into the war in Korea or not?

Yes 51%
No 35%
No opinion 14%

Americans became frustrated with the war which they had expected would be won. Many of them agreed with General MacArthur that the USA should aim for the kind of total victory over North Korea and China which they had achieved over Germany and Japan in 1945. But Truman wanted a negotiated settlement because he feared that the fighting might trigger off a third world war. In the end, negotiations for an armistice, which started in June 1951, brought the fighting to an end in a war in which neither side could claim to have achieved a decisive victory. It had been a costly war for the USA, with 54,000 men killed and over 100,000 wounded.

G The spread of nuclear weapons, 1945–1967

	Atomic bomb	Hydrogen bomb
USA	1945	1952
USSR	1949	1953
Britain	1952	1957
France	1960	1968
China	1964	1967

Containment

Not only had the Americans received a bloody nose in Korea, but their self-confidence as a superpower was further dented as they had lost their monopoly control of nuclear weapons.

United States' policy after the Korean War towards the Communists was one of containment, based largely on what appeared to be a 'balance of terror'. Presidents Truman, Eisenhower, and Kennedy, were determined to contain any further spread of Communism but also to avoid a war in which nuclear weapons on both sides would cause worldwide devastation. The US armed forces and those of allies such as NATO, with bases around the world, were built up so as to deter the Soviets or Chinese from advancing into any non-Communist countries. In a costly arms race, each side rapidly increased their arsenal of nuclear weapons, with the implicit threat that neither side would actually dare use them. The Cold War continued, with various crises that led to 'brinkmanship' by going to the verge of war, until the downfall of the Communist governments in the USSR and Eastern European countries began in 1989.

▼ The arms race

Events	USA	USSR
Atomic Bomb	1945	1949
Intercontinental Bomber	1948	1955
Alliances: NATO Warsaw Pact	1949	1955
H Bomb (Hydrogen bomb)	1952	1953
Intercontinental Ballistic Missile (ICBM)	1958	1957
Space Satellite	1958	1957
Submarine-launched Ballistic Missile (SLBM – Polaris)	1960	1968
First Man in Space	1962	1961

Neither could fly...
but they soloed to freedom

They had never flown before. But early one morning Zdne Machlúner, 19, and Karel Kucera, 20, tied up a Czech guard and wobbled to the safety of West Germany in a stolen plane.

These two escaped—but 70 million others remain captive behind the Iron Curtain. And these are the people at whom Radio Free Europe beams its daily broadcasts. Escape is not its aim. Radio Free Europe penetrates the Iron Curtain to spread truth ... to strengthen hope and resistance.

Said the youths above, "It (Radio Free Europe) added courage and strength to strained nerves."

"It offered us ... a hope for a better future," said a young nurse who fled to the West.

"Everybody is listening—even the Communists," said an escaped Czech skating champion.

From 29 powerful transmitters, Radio Free Europe broadcasts up to 20 hours of truth a day to five key satellite countries—Poland, Czechoslovakia, Romania, Hungary and Bulgaria. And how the Communist bosses fear it!

Each dollar you contribute sponsors a Minute of Truth on Radio Free Europe. How many minutes will you give?

Support Radio Free Europe • Send your Truth Dollars to: CRUSADE for FREEDOM c/o Local Postmaster

SPONSOR

H Radio Free Europe Poster

The Cold War took many forms, including the American financed radio stations, Radio Free Europe (1950) and the government's official station, Voice of America (1948). These broadcast news to inform people 'trapped' behind the 'Iron Curtain' and also to give them a taste of the American lifestyle including popular music. Radio Free Europe really broadcast propaganda but was very successful in undermining support among young people for the Communist system.

I

> Whether you like it or not, history is on our side. We will bury you.

Nikita Khrushchev, USSR Premier, made this threatening prophecy in November 1956

9 What was the cause of the war in Korea?
10 Why did most people not agree with Truman that it was simply a 'police action'?
11 Why did many Americans think the war in Korea was a mistake?
12 Why does the term 'balance of terror' effectively describe the Cold War during the 1950s?
13 Why were US backed radio stations an effective means of propaganda?

McCarthyism

One effect of the Cold War was an intense fear and hatred of Communism by most Americans, many of whom could not tell the difference between liberal or radical ideas and those of Communists. Communists or those thought to have sympathies in that direction, known as 'fellow-travellers', faced great intolerance and the loss of their political and other rights. 'Better dead than Red' became a patriotic slogan. The Communist Party of the USA, always small and ineffectual, was forced underground in the late 1940s after leading members were arrested. Congress set up the House Committee on Un-American Activities (HUAC) to investigate Communist involvement in the film industry, education unions and the government itself. Witnesses were supposed to prove their loyalty by publicly naming former Communists they had known, and if they didn't they could go to prison for 'contempt' and be blacklisted so that they couldn't get a job. A climate of intolerance that went far beyond the realms of reason was whipped up and damaged the lives, careers and civil liberties of many loyal Americans who were suspected by a gullible public of having Communist sympathies.

J Mike Hammer's view of Communists

> I killed more people tonight than I have fingers on my hands. I shot them in cold blood and enjoyed every minute of it... they were Commies. They were Red sons-of-bitches who should have died long ago... They never thought that there were people like me in this country. They figured us all to be soft as horse manure and just as stupid.

These are the words of Mike Hammer, private detective, a character created by novelist Mickey Spillane, from the book *One Lonely Night* which appeared in 1951 and which sold three million copies

The name of Senator Joe McCarthy has been given to the campaign against Communists that caught up and ruined so many who were innocent of any Communist sympathies. McCarthy embarked on a campaign based essentially on smears, exaggerations, and downright lies that propelled himself into the limelight as the leader of patriotic Americans determined to root out Communist traitors. Joe McCarthy alleged that Communists had gained high positions in government and even in the Military.

Senator McCarthy's allegation that senior officials were aware that a large number of Communists were working in the government was quite sensational. But McCarthy kept altering the figure, and when he announced there were actually fifty-seven Communists working in the State Department, one magazine derided it as the 'Heinz varieties figure'. In fact McCarthy provided no evidence to back up his allegations and never uncovered a single Communist agent in the government. Even so, particularly with the Korean War going on, there were many people prepared to believe him and some prominent politicians chose to support him. Other politicians, including the President, were reluctant to criticise him. 'The Senate', said one newspaper, 'is afraid of him'.

In the end, McCarthy simply went too far and began to attack officers in the US Army. A Senate sub-committee held televised hearings that were watched by millions to investigate his charges and gradually public opinion began to turn against him. The hearings exposed McCarthy's behaviour and irresponsibility to the scrutiny of the TV audience and finally discredited him. In the White House, President Eisenhower joked to his Cabinet, 'Have you heard the latest? McCarthyism is McCarthywasm.'

K McCarthyism

1 The political practice of publicizing accusations of disloyalty or subversion with insufficient regard to evidence.
2 The use of methods of investigation and accusation regarded as unfair in order to suppress opposition.

The definition of 'McCarthyism' in *The American Heritage Dictionary*

L 'I have a list...'

While I cannot take the time to name all the men in the State Department who have been named as members of the Communist Party and members of a spy ring, I have here in my hand a list of 205 that are known to the Secretary of State as being members of the Communist Party and are still working and shaping the policy of the State Department.

Part of the speech by Senator Joe McCarthy to the Ohio County Women's Club in Wheeling, West Virginia, in January 1950

M Herblock cartoon

"I HAVE HERE IN MY HAND—"

This 1954 cartoon in the Washington Post seemed to sum up McCarthy's methods. 'I have here in my hand' from Herblock's *Here and Now* (Simon and Schuster, 1955)

N 'See it now'

This is no time for men who oppose Senator McCarthy's methods to keep silent... We proclaim ourselves – as indeed we are – the defenders of freedom, what's left of it, but we cannot defend freedom abroad by deserting it at home. The actions of the junior Senator from Wisconsin have caused alarm and dismay... he didn't create the situation of fear; he merely exploited it, and rather successfully.

Ed Murrow used these words at the close of the *See It Now* TV programme shown across the nation on the CBS network, which exposed McCarthy's methods of half-truth and distortion

14 Source J is taken from a novel. Do novels such as this provide historians with any useful historical evidence?
15 Which sources support the view of the cartoonist in Source M?
16 Why would many politicians have been reluctant to criticise McCarthy?
17 Explain how Sources L–N help to explain the definition of 'McCarthyism' in Source K.
18 What do you think McCarthy meant when he said, 'McCarthyism is Americanism with its sleeves rolled up'?

▼ Senator Joe McCarthy

O Patriotic

Senator McCarthy was a patriotic American and a determined opponent of Communists. And because of that every 'liberal' commentator lost no opportunity to villify him... No man in public life was ever persecuted and maligned because of his beliefs as was Senator McCarthy.

Chicago Tribune, May 1957, following the death of McCarthy

The military-industrial complex

P Misplaced power

We have been compelled to create a permanent armaments industry of vast proportions. Added to this, three and a half million men and women are directly engaged in the defense establishment... Now this conjunction of an immense military establishment and a large arms industry is new in the American experience... In the councils of government, we must guard against the acquisition of unwarranted influence, whether sought or unsought, by the military-industrial complex. The potential for the disastrous rise of misplaced power exists and will persist.

President Eisenhower in his Farewell Address in January 1960. Eisenhower had a distinguished career in the army before entering politics and was well aware of the way the military operated.

The massive expenditure on the arms race benefited a few large industrial corporations, such as General Electric and General Motors. President Eisenhower warned that a coalition of private companies and the military establishment, which he called the 'military-industrial complex' (MIC), might exercise too much political influence.

19 Explain the meaning of the term 'military-industrial complex'.
20 Why was President Eisenhower concerned about the MIC?

Essay:
a Explain the meaning of the term 'Cold War' to describe post-war relations between the USA and USSR.
b How was America affected by the fear of Communism between 1945–1960?

Further research: Examine crises and cases of 'brinkmanship' during the Cold War.

10 America in the 1950s
The affluent society

During the years 1945–1970, Americans enjoyed unprecedented prosperity, as rapid economic growth provided most middle-class white Americans with a comfortable lifestyle that was envied around the world. Between 1945 and 1960, a post-war 'baby boom' increased the population by about 40 million, an increase of 30%, to a total 179,323,175. During the same period the gross national product (GNP), which is the total value of all the goods and services produced in one year, almost doubled and during the 1950s the USA was producing half of the world's goods. As people became more affluent many of them moved to new homes in well-planned and self-contained suburban communities, complete with new shopping centres called malls. In turn, the inner cities began a spiral of decline as fewer well off people lived, shopped or even worked there. Cars, TVs, refrigerators, and washing machines, together with countless other gadgets previously thought of as luxuries, came to be considered as simple every-day necessities. Owning a car or the latest HiFi record player, or perhaps installing a swimming pool, became important status symbols in suburbia. The invention of the transistor, which replaced large and costly valves in such things as radios and televisions, revolutionised the manufacture of electric circuits. By 1960, 90% of homes had television sets, which changed the pattern of daily life and was blamed for many social ills, including increased juvenile crime. Almost all television stations were commercial and 20 % of broadcasting time was taken up by commercials, far more than was permitted in Britain.

The term 'consumerism' describes the theory that this steadily increasing purchase of goods, not only makes people happy, but ensures growth in the economy. Hire purchase, known as consumer credit, increased by 800% between 1945 and 1957. Whereas people in other industrial countries, such as Britain, saved between 5–10% of their income, by 1960 Americans were only saving 5%. In 1960 the standard of living of the average American was three times that of the average Briton. They were encouraged to spend and shopping became a popular recreational activity. President Eisenhower, a Republican committed to free enterprise, who served from 1953 until 1961, once advised people during a slight drop in sales to 'buy anything'. Teenagers had more money to spend on themselves than their parents had ever had during the years of Depression and war and were certainly better off than young people in other countries. For the first time teenage fads and fashions were profitable, with products such as transistor radios, magazines, rock 'n' roll records and Elvis movies. Those who had lived through the 1930s now recognised that the country was well and truly out of Depression. The so-called 'baby boomers' who grew up in the 1950s would later, in the 1960s–1980s, look back on the 1950s as a period of 'peace and prosperity'.

Statistics of prosperity

A Unemployment, 1947–63

Percentage of the labour force unemployed					
1947	3.9%	1953	2.9%	1959	5.5%
1948	3.75%	1954	5.5%	1960	5.5%
1949	5.9%	1955	4.4%	1961	6.7%
1950	5.3%	1956	4.1%	1962	5.5%
1951	3.3%	1957	4.3%	1963	5.6%
1952	3.0%	1958	6.8%		

Unemployment had reached 25% in 1933 and was still over 10% in 1941. Even so, it began to rise during the late 1950s and although the percentage figures appear relatively low, the 1958 figure still represents 2,859,000 people.

B Consumer goods in American families, 1948–1956
(Source: US Department of Commerce)

		Families owning (%)		
	Cars	Televisions	Refrigerators	Washing machines
1948	54.0	2.9	76.6	67.4
1949	56.0	10.1	79.2	68.6
1950	60.0	26.4	86.4	71.9
1951	65.0	38.5	86.7	73.5
1952	65.0	50.2	89.2	76.2
1953	65.0	63.5	90.4	78.5
1954	70.0	74.1*	92.5	81.3
1955	71.0	76.1	94.1	84.1
1956	73.0	81.0	96.0	86.8

(* in Britain only 4%)

	1950	1960
Home owners	23,600,000	32,800,000
Hot dog sales (lbs)	750,000,000	1050,000,000
Little Leagues (baseball for children)	776	5,700
Power lawn mowers	1,000,000	3,000,000
Gallons of gin	6,000,000	19,000,000
Aspirin sales (lbs)	12,000,000	18,000,000

D Average wages of factory workers
(Source: US Department of Labor)

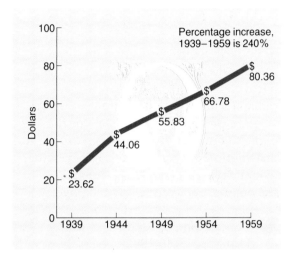

Percentage increase, 1939–1959 is 240%

$23.62 (1939), $44.06 (1944), $55.83 (1949), $66.78 (1954), $80.36 (1959)

E

This 1957 car advertisement displayed the glamorous and affluent side of American life that was idealised all over the world. More than anything else, American cars seemed to represent the enduring success of the American free-enterprise system.

8 big advances make the 1957

DE SOTO

the most exciting car in the world today!

C Life in the Fifties

Movies and magazines carried the news of American success to millions of envious people around the world. Vast supermarkets, new freeways, rock 'n' roll music, large cars with fins and chrome, and television game shows were all, so it was claimed, symbols of a flourishing economy and a free society. One economist called it 'galloping capitalism', and a member of President Eisenhower's Cabinet revealingly said, 'What's good for General Motors is good for the country'.

1 Explain how the term 'consumerism' describes the 1950s.
2 What effect did the growth of the suburbs have on the cities?
3 What can we learn about life in America from Sources A–D?
4 What are the strengths and weaknesses of statistical evidence?
5 What aspects of American life would people in other countries have been likely to admire?

The other Americans

Not everyone was impressed with this free-for-all which allowed large corporations to make immense profits and many individuals to do well, whilst neglecting important aspects of community life. Many Americans, particularly but not exclusively blacks, remained an underclass who were unable to share in the prosperity. In spite of the highest standard of living in the world, the distribution of wealth was so uneven that in 1959 the government said that 22% of the population lived below the poverty level.

F The income of black and white families, 1950–1962

	(median income*)	
	Black	**White**
1950	$3,828	$7,057
1953	$4,547	$8,110
1956	$4,768	$9,060
1959	$5,348	$9,970
1962	$5,429	$10,168

(* median income is the amount which divides the distribution into two equal groups, so that an equal number of families are above and below each figure.) The US Bureau of Labor calculated in 1950 that a family income of $3,717 was necessary to maintain a family of four on a modest but adequate basis.

People's income was also affected by the area of the country in which they lived. People in the southern states, in particular, remained well behind those in the North or on the West Coast. Some of the poorest were in the Mississippi clay hills, where in 1960 more than 60% of families tried to live on less than $2,000 a year. Most elderly people who had endured two world wars and the Depression failed to benefit from the booming economy. In 1960, 67.8% of persons over the age of sixty-five had incomes of less than $1,000 and 94.3% of them had less than $3,000. Of course many of them had fewer demands on their money than younger people with families, but they generally had higher medical bills and the cost of medical care rose very rapidly. The US lagged far behind European countries in providing good pensions and welfare services. Despite a booming economy and evidence that medical care was costly and inadequate, Congress defeated attempts to set up a comprehensive national health service. Opposition to improved welfare came from powerful and politically influential insurance companies, and from those who argued that welfarism would undermine the traditional 'rugged individualism' of Americans. But critics, inside and outside the USA, attacked this contradiction of American society with its great wealth and consumerism on the one hand, but significant poverty and lack of social provision on the other.

G Best dressed poverty

America has the best dressed poverty the world has ever known... It is much easier in the United States to be decently dressed than it is to be decently housed, fed or doctored... At precisely that moment in history where for the first time a people have the material ability to end poverty, they lack the will to do so. They cannot see, they cannot act, the consciences of the well-off are the victims of affluence ...

Michael Harrington, an American academic and political activist, in *The Other America* (1962), strongly attacked the unequal distribution of America's wealth and the failure of the government to make sure that everyone had proper medical care when they needed it

H The affluent society

The family which takes its mauve and cerise, air-conditioned, power-steered, and power-braked automobile out for a tour, passes through cities that are badly paved, made hideous by litter, blighted buildings, billboards, and posts for wires that should long since have been put underground. They pass into a countryside that has been rendered invisible by commercial art (advertising hoardings). They picnic on exquisitely packaged food from a portable icebox by a polluted stream... Is this American genius?

Harvard economics professor, John Kenneth Galbraith, wrote *The Affluent Society* (1958), in which he criticised the consumer society and argued for more public spending on schools, hospitals, cultural activities, and social services

How can we talk about prosperity to the sick who cannot afford proper medical care, to the mentally ill for whom there is no room in our over-crowded institutions? How can we talk about prosperity to the hundreds of thousands who can find no decent place to live at prices they can afford? And how can we talk about prosperity to a share-cropper living on worn-out land, or to city-dwellers packed six to a room in an unlit tenement with a garbage-strewn alley for their children's playground? To these people, national prosperity is a mockery – to the eleven million families in this nation with incomes of less than $2,000 a year.

Part of a speech in 1952 by Adlai Stevenson, a Democrat who unsuccessfully stood twice against Eisenhower in the presidential elections. Of course, action against the problems identified by Stevenson would have meant higher taxes for other people.

J The Soviet View

American capitalist telling an unemployed man, 'Get away – you're spoiling the whole show!' This Russian cartoon points out that even in the affluent society of the USA there were many people suffering poverty and unemployment.

The Communist countries were quick to seize on any shortcomings in America, to point out that beneath the surface glitter were serious social problems and that in reality life in the USA was not as it appeared in the movies or in advertisements. Both the USA and USSR were eager to persuade people elsewhere in the world that their own society was better than the other one.

6 What is the significance of the information in Source F?
7 Assess the reliability of each of the sources F-J.
8 How widespread was poverty?
9 What evidence is there in this chapter which the Soviets, as in Source J, might have used to criticise the American system of private enterprise?
10 Why do you think the government did not do more to eradicate poverty?

Religion in the Fifties

One aspect of middle-class suburban life was the rapid growth of church and synagogue congregations. Various reasons for this can be considered. The Cold War threat to the USA from atheist Communists led some people, including Federal Bureau of Investigation (FBI) director, J. Edgar Hoover, to encourage parents to take their children to church as a defence against the spread of Communism. Another reason was that joining organisations helped replace the friendships and sense of community left behind when people moved to the suburbs. Churches provided immediate friendship and countless social opportunities in a respectable and secure environment. By 1960 more than 65% of adults were regularly attending church compared with less than 50% in 1940.

President Eisenhower also stressed the value of God, whom he called the 'Supreme Being', and in 1954 Congress added the words 'one nation under God' to the Pledge of Allegiance, and the following year made the phrase 'In God We trust' mandatory on all US currency. Some people worried that the idea of separation

The magnetic fervour of Billy Graham made him the most famous evangelist preacher

A woman's place was in the kitchen according to advertisements such as this. Whereas men purchased cars suburban women supposedly coveted a fitted kitchen with all the latest gadgets.

of Church and State (see chapter 2) was being eroded, but they were reassured by controversial decisions by the Supreme Court in 1962 and 1963 that prayers and bible readings in public schools were unconstitutional.

Religious organisations were quick to employ the same marketing methods that businesses were so successfully using. Advertising hoardings and TV commercials carried such messages as, 'a family that prays together stays together'. Evangelists purchased time on TV and radio to broadcast Christian programmes and services which linked elements of entertainment with powerful sermons and appeals for donations. The most successful, Billy Graham, became a close friend of

several Presidents and conducted huge 'crusades', including a highly publicised one in England in 1954. Graham and others reassured people that the American free enterprise way of life and their leadership of the 'free world', backed up by a growing arsenal of nuclear weapons, was all in keeping with the teaching of the Bible. They provided a moral defence of the affluent society.

11 How does the growth of affluence in the 1950s help to explain the increase in Church membership?
12 Why do you think fairly well-off people wanted a moral or religious support for their affluent way of life?

A woman's place in the Fifties

Within a few years of the end of the war, women's wages in factories, which had risen to two-thirds of those earned by men, fell back to 53% of men's. Much of the equality gained during the war gave way to the more traditional roles for men and women. Although the dominant view was that a woman's place was in the home, the needs of the consumer society dictated that women should go out to work in order to

be able to help their husbands buy the gadgets now thought essential for a decent life. But although more women were going out to work than ever before, 40% by 1960, most of them were in stereotyped 'women's occupations' on low wages, such as office and shop work.

K The ideal woman, 1956

Life magazine described the 'ideal' woman as being, 'a thirty-two year old pretty and popular suburban housewife, mother of four, who had married at age sixteen, an excellent wife, mother, hostess, volunteer, and home manager who makes her own clothes, hosts dozens of dinner parties each year, sings in the church choir, works with the school PTA and Campfire Girls and is devoted to her husband. In her daily round she attends club or charity meetings, drives the children to school, does the weekly grocery shopping, makes ceramics, and is planning to study French. Of all the accomplishments of the American woman the one she brings off with the most spectacular success is having babies'.

Extract from Life magazine, 1956

"lucky because upkeep is child's play in our gay Republic Steel Kitchen deftly arranged to help us live the good life. Steel is so practical! It won't shrink, warp, swell or sag ... remains the same through every season, in every climate. It won't harbor vermin, mildew or unwanted odors. And Republic, pioneer in steel kitchens, brings you a line full of fresh, uncopied ideas, with dozens of features and work-easing conveniences to make your new or remodeled kitchen a joy forever. Your dealer has them on display."

The institution of marriage, whether based on the hope of fulfillment or the fear of loneliness, was sacrosanct in the Fifties. Everybody got married... Marriage was celebrated as a state of bliss. So, too, was having children. In diaper (nappy) ads babies always smiled and never cried. Child-rearing was depicted as an exciting challenge rather than as an ordinary chore. Indeed, housewifely tasks were glorified as proof of the 'complete' woman: chef, hostess, nurse, laundress, maid, story-teller, shopper, PTA member, flower planter, interior decorator, not to mention chauffeur at the call of children at the playground or the husband at the railroad station... Many high school girls were more desirous of securing a husband than a college degree... If there was a women's movement in the Fifties, it led directly to the wedding chapel.

'State of bliss'

John Patrick Diggins, a professor of history at the University of California, in *The Proud Decades*, 1988

▶

The phenomenon of Elvis Presley swept the country and then the world in 1956. To the young he was the 'King' but most adults detested his rebellious sexuality.

13 How does Source K explain the role of women in the 1950s?
14 Do you think that Source L is biased?
15 'If suburban women enjoyed their lives primarily as wives and mothers, did it matter that fewer were gaining university degrees or pursuing careers?' Discuss this proposition.

Youth Culture

Young people in the 1950s had far more money to spend on themselves than any previous generation of teenagers had had, and companies responded with new products specifically targetted towards them. In 1957 it was estimated that the average teenager had between $10–$15 a week to spend, compared with $1–$2 in the early 1940s. Teenagers' annual spending power climbed from $10 billion in 1950 to $25 billion by 1959. The Allstate Insurance Company found that 75% of High School boys aged 16–17 had a driver's licence and the car played a vital part in young people's lives.

In 1956, Elvis Presley erupted onto the pop music scene, singing songs that broke all sales records, such as *Heartbreak Hotel* and *Hound Dog*. That year record sales were 90 million, and 10 million were by Elvis. Elvis was a phenomenal success with teenagers, whilst their parents and teachers deplored his sensual style of performing, his long sideburns and permanent sneer. It was claimed that this Rock 'n' Roll music

encouraged teenage crime. Teenagers everywhere, including the Communist countries, quickly copied these fashions so that Elvis became an international symbol that united young people and ensured that America was the dominant influence in the world's popular music. For all the criticisms, the adults who owned and operated the record, movie and television companies, were quick to encourage and satisfy this profitable market.

Other young people 'dropped out' of conventional society altogether to become 'Beatniks'. Jack Kerouac's 1957 novel, *On the Road*, chronicling free sexual behaviour and rejection of parental morality, appealed to young and rebellious intellectuals. For many older Americans it was difficult to understand or tolerate this 'generation gap'.

16 Who might have resented the new purchasing power of teenagers?
17 Why did America lead the way to teenagers all over the world in music and fashions?
18 How does the evidence in this chapter help to explain the popularity of President Eisenhower?
19 The 1950s is sometimes described as the 'placid decade'. Do you think this is an appropriate term?
Essay: Was the USA really an 'affluent society' in the 1950s?
Further research: Find out about the life and presidency of President Eisenhower and his Vice President, Richard Nixon.

11 Black Americans
Segregation is challenged

The racist system of segregation remained firmly in place at the end of the Second World War in the southern states (see map), as well as in Washington DC. 'Negroes', wrote one historian, 'still did not exist as people for mainstream America'. Apart from the fact that they did many of the menial jobs, they were largely ignored by the rest of America. Segregation meant separate restaurant and entertainment facilities, separate waiting rooms in bus stations, even separate launderettes and drinking fountains. The most seriously detrimental effect resulted from the segregated education system. In 1954 twenty states, as well as Washington DC, had legally enforced segregated schools under the so-called 'separate but equal' doctrine that was the basis of segregation. But separate schools were never equal and the schools provided for black children were always inferior to those for whites, so that black pupils were denied an equal educational opportunity. 'Segregation', the National Association for the Advancement of Colored People (NAACP) declared, 'is the way in which a society tells a group of human beings that they are inferior to the other groups'.

▲ In 1954, twenty states as well as Washington DC had segregated schools

Brown v. Board of Education of Topeka, 1954

The NAACP challenged the right of the local school boards, including the one in Topeka, Kansas, to run segregated schools. On 17 May 1954, the Supreme Court reached the unanimous and momentous decision that segregation in education was illegal under the Constitution.

▼ The Supreme Court decision

To separate (Negro children) from others of similar age and qualifications, solely because of their race, generates a feeling of inferiority as to their status in the community that may affect their hearts and minds in a way never to be undone... We conclude that in the field of public education the doctrine of 'separate but equal' has no place. Separate educational facilities are inherently unequal.

These were the words of the Chief Justice, Earl Warren, on Monday 17 May 1954, which signalled the end of school segregation because it was contrary to the Constitution of the USA

President Eisenhower was not pleased with the Court's decision because, although he supported racial integration, he knew how stubborn southern whites were, and he favoured a gradual process of breaking down racial barriers. Privately he said that his appointment of Earl Warren to the Court was 'the biggest damn-fool mistake I ever made'. Publicly he declared his responsibility as head of the federal government: 'The Constitution is as the Supreme Court interprets it and I must do my very best to see that it is carried out'.

The following year the Supreme Court ruled that the states had to comply with their ruling and get on with integrating their schools. But southern whites were furiously determined not to give way. Diehard segregationists called it 'Black Monday' and one southern senator, Harry F. Byrd, provided a fighting slogan when he urged, 'massive resistance'. Southern states fell back on the argument of 'states rights', that each state had the right to decide such matters for themselves. By the end of 1956, in six southern states not a single black child was attending a school with white children, and in the other states only small steps had been taken towards integration.

Why did the South cling so defiantly to the system of segregation and why did so many southerners treat black people so badly? Even when the Supreme Court had ruled that segregation was unlawful, southerners, including state governments and police forces, resisted integration so that violence and deaths resulted. The Ku Klux Klan organised poor whites in rural areas whilst the self-appointed Citizen's Councils recruited middle-class people. Responses to the Supreme Court's ruling ranged from deliberate inaction and obstinacy by school boards to riots, bombings and even the murder of NAACP supporters.

Lynchings and beatings which had declined since the 1920s increased again. In 1955, fourteen year old Emmett Till, from Chicago, was brutally murdered while staying with relatives in Mississippi.

Unused to southern ways and the extent of bigotry, Emmett unwisely had been cheeky to a young white woman. Those believed to be responsible were acquitted by an all-white jury. But the impact of Emmett's murder, and the failure to punish those responsible, was enormous and focused attention on the injustice and violence that black people in the South had to face; his mother described her dead son as 'a little nobody who shook up the world'.

White racial prejudice in opposition to desegregation was shown in the most extreme form by the Ku Klux Klan. They were responsible for many crimes of murder, violence and intimidation of black fellow Americans.

A The southern view

... when a law transgresses the moral and ethical sanctions and standards of the mores (customs), invariably strife, bloodshed and revolution follow in the wake of its attempted enforcement. The loveliest and purest of God's creatures, the nearest thing to an angelic being that treads this terrestrial ball is a well-bred, cultured southern white woman or her blue-eyed, golden-haired little girl... We say to the Supreme Court and to the northern world, 'You shall not make us drink from this cup'... We have, through our forefathers, died before for our sacred principles. We can, if necessary, die again.

Tom Brady, a judge in the southern state of Mississippi, wrote this in his book *Black Monday* to justify opposition to the Supreme Court ruling. He reminded his readers that their forefathers had died fighting in the Civil War.

B Fear

Before Emmett Till's murder, I had known the fear of hunger, hell and the Devil. But now there was a new fear known to me – the fear of being killed just because I was black. This was the worst of my fears... I didn't know what one had to do or not to do as a Negro not to be killed. Probably just being a Negro was enough, I thought.

This was how a fourteen year old black girl, Anne Moody, who lived in Mississippi in 1955, felt when she heard about the murder of Emmett Till

1 What reasons did the Supreme Court give for their decision against segregation?
2 How do Sources A and B help to explain President Eisenhower's concern over the Supreme Court decision?
3 What effect do you think the murder of Emmett Till had on public opinion?

The bus boycott

Segregation on buses was a petty indignity endured by black people every day. In Montgomery, Alabama, on 1 December 1955, a forty-two year old black woman, Rosa Parks, refused the order of a bus driver to give up her seat to a white male and stand at the rear of the bus as was required by law. She was arrested and fined $10. But within forty-eight hours her angry friends and family had staged a twenty-four hour bus boycott that was so successful that they decided to continue it until the bus company agreed to seat all passengers on a first-come basis. Since black passengers accounted for about 75% of the bus company's business, the boycott was extremely damaging. But with segregation under attack, the company, backed by the Mayor and most of the white community, refused to back down. In spite of the great inconvenience, the black community remained united and determined with their slogan, 'People don't ride the bus today. Don't ride it for freedom'. One of those who led the campaign was a young black minister, Dr Martin Luther King, who believed that mass non-violent protest was the best way to resist injustice.

▲ This photograph of Rosa Parks was taken after the successful campaign against bus segregation, so that she and other black people could sit wherever they wished

D Klansmen in Montgomery

By walking in the streets of Montgomery wearing their robes, these Klansmen probably hoped to frighten blacks into ending their boycott of the buses and to accept segregation. But this kind of demonstration of so-called white superiority, that had proved effective in the past, was now fast becoming obsolete.

C

'a great people'

Martin Luther King made this speech in Montgomery in 1955. He became the most important civil rights leader and in 1964 he was awarded the Nobel Peace Prize. Tragically, he was murdered in 1968 whilst supporting a strike by Memphis refuse workers.

There comes a time when people get tired – tired of being segregated and humiliated; tired of being kicked about by the brutal feet of oppression... For many years we have shown amazing patience. We have sometimes given our white brothers the feeling that we liked the way we are being treated... One of the great glories of democracy is the right to protest for right... if you will protest courageously and yet with dignity and Christian love, when the history books are written in future generations, the historians will pause and say, 'There lived a great people – a black people – who injected new meaning and dignity into the veins of civilization'. That is our challenge and our overwhelming responsibility.

Tension increased as the boycott continued and the homes of leading blacks were attacked, including the bombing of King's home where his wife and seven week old baby narrowly escaped injury. Whites, appalled by this threat to segregation, flocked to join the local Citizen's Council.

In November 1956, the Supreme Court ruled that segregation on buses was illegal and on 20 December, nearly thirteen months after the boycott began, the bus company gave in and black Americans were able to celebrate a victory that attracted worldwide attention.

4   What did the slogan of the bus boycott, 'Don't ride it for freedom' mean?
5   What did Dr King mean, in Source C, by the phrase 'great people'?
6   In what ways were the people of Montgomery divided over the issue of the bus boycott?

Little Rock

The inevitable confrontation between the US Government and southern segregationists finally occurred in Little Rock, the state capital of Arkansas. President Eisenhower was prepared to act decisively over an issue that deeply divided Americans.

E Gallup opinion poll, 13 January 1957

The United States Supreme Court has ruled that racial segregation in the public schools is illegal. This means that all children, no matter what their race, must be allowed to go to the same schools.
Do you approve or disapprove of this decision?

Entire USA	Approve	63%
	Disapprove	31%
	No opinion	6%
South only	Approve	27%
	Disapprove	67%
	No opinion	6%

The Governor of Arkansas used the National Guard, reserve soldiers under the control of the local state, to prevent nine black pupils from enrolling at the Little Rock High School, even though the law said that they could. Faced with further court action, the Governor withdrew the Guard and then left the young teenagers unprotected from a violent mob of white students and adults who surrounded the school, determined to prevent the blacks from entering the previously all-white school. Faced with this dangerous situation, Eisenhower sent in one thousand US paratroopers, many with fixed bayonets, to protect the small number of black students as they attended school for the next twelve months. The fact that heavily armed troops were necessary if black and white children were to attend school together, was clear evidence of the deep-rooted racial hatred and discrimination that existed.

Elizabeth Eckford

This photograph shows fifteen year old Elizabeth Eckford on her way to the previously all-white school in Little Rock in September 1957

G 'Respect for law'

I have today issued an Executive Order directing the use of troops under federal authority to aid in the execution of federal law at Little Rock, Arkansas... The very basis of our individual rights and freedoms rests upon the certainty that the President and the Executive Branch of Government will support and insure the carrying out of the decisions of the federal courts, even, when necessary with all the means at the President's command... Mob rule cannot be allowed to override the decisions of our courts... The overwhelming majority of our people in every section of the country are united in their respect for observance of the law – even in those cases where they may disagree with that law ...
It would be difficult to exaggerate the harm that is being done to the prestige and influence, and indeed to the safety, of our nation and the world.
Our enemies are gloating over this incident and using it everywhere to misrepresent our whole nation.

On 24 September 1959, President Eisenhower dispatched troops to Little Rock to protect the admission of the black pupils, and then went on television to explain his action

People in other countries criticised the USA for failing to live up to the commitment contained in the US Declaration of Independence that: 'all men are created equal' with the right to 'life, liberty and the pursuit of happiness'.

In spite of Eisenhower's commitment to enforcing the law in Little Rock, most forms of segregation remained. New laws such as the *Civil Rights Act* of 1957, the first such law since 1875, and later ones in the 1960s made discrimination illegal and endeavoured to guarantee the vital right to vote. Nevertheless, by the end of the 1950s many black Americans thought the civil rights movement had failed, and increasingly demanded more militant action.

The threat of violence was so serious that President Eisenhower ordered heavily armed soldiers to escort nine black pupils into the Little Rock Central High School. Pictures such as this appeared in newspapers all over the world.

H

LITTLE ROCK CENTRAL HI

7 How does Source E help explain the problem that President Eisenhower faced?

8 What can we learn about race relations in Little Rock from Sources F and H?

9 How might the events in Little Rock have been used to damage America's prestige?

10 Is there any evidence in any of the sources that justifies Eisenhower's use of the word 'mob'?

11 Why were the events in Little Rock so important?

12 Explain the likely impact of each of the sources in this chapter on
  i white southerners
  ii black people.

Essay:
 i Explain the reactions of Americans to the campaign against segregation in the 1950s.
 ii 'It was the Supreme Court that helped black Americans and not their protests'. How true is that statement?

Further research: Find out about the philosophy of non-violent protest and civil disobedience advocated by Dr Martin Luther King and find other examples of how they were used to resist racial discrimination.

12 Kennedy
The New Frontier

In 1960 the USA enjoyed a strong economic, military and political position that was virtually unchallenged. Nevertheless, problems and issues that had begun to emerge during the 1950s were to cause deep divisions and turmoil during the 1960s. The government had no doubt that prosperity would continue and that there was broad consensus support for their form of government, together with the private enterprise economy. A 1960 presidential commission, *Goals for Americans*, saw no cause for concern about the nation's future, and expected prosperity and political stability to continue.

Yet there were potentially divisive issues facing America:

- Civil rights: black or African Americans were becoming more and more frustrated and impatient with the slow progress being made in dismantling segregation and in achieving equal rights.
- Urban decline: inner city ghettos of unemployment, poverty, and rising crime characterised all the major cities.
- Foreign policy: the arms race that had resulted from the Cold War continued, and the USA was increasingly challenged by the USSR in Europe, Asia and even in the Caribbean by the USSR's protege, Cuba.

'A new generation'

In November 1960 a new President, John Kennedy, a Democrat, was elected to succeed President Eisenhower. Kennedy was the first Roman Catholic to be elected, a fact that was quite a controversial issue in 1960. He was also the youngest ever President when he took office at the age of 43, and much of his support came from younger people.

Kennedy described himself as an 'idealist without illusions' and he knew that having won with only a wafer-thin majority, he had no mandate that he could use against the conservatives who controlled Congress and who were opposed to his plans to extend welfare benefits.

John Kennedy had great style that charmed, captivated, and inspired people around the world to have faith that government could solve many problems and that working in the public service was worthwhile. During his presidency many young educated people decided to pursue careers in government or to get involved in politics or to join the Peace Corps, which sent thousands of skilled young people to help in underdeveloped nations. A Peace Corps volunteer said in 1962: 'I'd never done anything political, patriotic or unselfish, because nobody ever asked me to. Kennedy asked'.

1960 Presidential election result

John Kennedy
34,227,096
Democrat
49.7%

Richard Nixon
34,108,546
Republican
49.5%

A 'the torch has been passed...'

Let the word go forth from this time and place, to friend and foe alike, that the torch has been passed to a new generation of Americans – born in this century, tempered by war, disciplined by a hard and bitter peace... Let every nation know whether it wishes us well or ill, that we shall pay any price, bear any burden, meet any hardship, support any friend, oppose any foe to assure survival and success of liberty...

To those nations who would make themselves our adversary, we offer not a pledge but a request: that both sides begin anew the quest for peace, before the dark powers of destruction unleashed by science engulf all humanity in planned or accidental self-destruction...

And so, my fellow Americans: ask not what your country can do for you, ask what you can do for your country.

Part of President Kennedy's inaugural speech in January 1961 in which he set out his ideas for what was called the 'New Frontier'

1 What did Kennedy mean in his speech (Source A) by the phrase 'disciplined by a hard and bitter peace'?

2 Is there any evidence in Source A to support the view that the speech was 'inspiring'?

3 Was it wise of Kennedy to make the kind of promises he gave in Source A?

Confrontation with the USSR

Tension between the USA and USSR continued into the 1960s, and there were occasions when it seemed that Cold War brinkmanship might spill over into a real war. Both of these 'superpowers' confronted one another with an increasing number of nuclear weapons as well as a massive conventional arsenal. Through a constant stream of propaganda, including radio stations broadcasting to each others populations, insults and threats were exchanged. Each side in these Cold War arguments claimed the superiority of their political and economic systems. They were desperate to gain more influence for themselves over other nations and to curb the spread of the other's influence. The great fear among both politicians and the public was that a confrontation between the USA and USSR could change the Cold War into a real all-out shooting war. There were several possible flash-points where tension was high. These included Berlin, Cuba and South East Asia.

B Superpower confrontation

	USA	USSR
ICBM	450	76
MRBM	250	700
Bombers	2260	1600
Tanks	16 000	38 000
Submarines		
nuclear	32	12
conventional	260	495
Cruisers	66	30
escorts	1107	189
Battleships and carriers	76	nil

The military strength of the USA and USSR in 1962

C Kennedy's view of Communism

Where we feel the difficulty comes is the effort by the Soviet Union to communise, in a sense, the entire world... We want the people of the Soviet Union to live in peace – we want the same for our own people. It is this effort to push outward the Communist system, on to country after country, that represents, I think, the great threat to peace. If the Soviet Union looked only to its national interest and to providing a better life for its people under conditions of peace, I think there would be nothing that would disturb the relations between the Soviet Union and the United States.

President Kennedy in an interview with the editor of *Izvestia*, a Soviet newspaper, on 28 November 1961

Berlin crisis

The city of Berlin was marooned in the middle of Communist East Germany. After the Second World War, Berlin was divided between Britain, France, the USA, and the USSR. The Soviet sector became the capital of East Germany. The other sectors joined together to form West Berlin. The Soviets constantly sought to remove the western powers altogether from Berlin so that the entire city could be part of East Germany. West Berliners had a far higher standard of living and more political freedom than did the East Berliners. West Berlin's well-stocked shops, and radio and TV Stations with their western programmes, were a constant irritation to East German Communists and their Soviet ally. The issue in Soviet minds was to what extent the USA and their NATO allies would go to protect West Berlin.

The USA had three basic objectives:

a the freedom of West Berliners to choose their own system of government;

b the continued presence of US, British and French troops, so long as West Berliners wanted them to stay;

c free access through East Germany to West Berlin by road, canal, and air.

American support for West Berlin was intended to demonstrate a firm stand against any spread of Communist power. The USSR had to decide whether or not the US was bluffing or was in fact prepared to go to war – possibly a nuclear world war – in defence of their part of the city.

In June 1961 President Kennedy met the Soviet leader Nikita Khrushchev in Vienna. Khrushchev told Kennedy that the USSR was absolutely determined that the entire city of Berlin should become part of East Germany. Kennedy warned that any Soviet invasion would be strongly resisted. Force, Kennedy said, would be met by force. Even so, the Soviets seemed to think that the young President would not actually go to war. The Soviet ambassador to the USA was reported as saying 'when the chips are down, the United States won't fight for Berlin'.

President Kennedy was, however, determined to hold on to West Berlin. 'All Europe', he said, 'is at stake in West Berlin'. He increased the military budget, called up more men to serve in the army and mobilised 158,000 reserve soldiers. Additional troops were sent to Berlin and West Germany ready to oppose any invasion.

In August 1961 the USSR dramatically raised the tension into a crisis. A wall was hastily constructed between East and West Berlin. The Berlin Wall prevented East and West Berliners from visiting each others parts of the city. Families and friends were separated. Force was used to stop anyone trying to leave East Berlin, and some people were shot. The Berlin Wall came to be a symbol of repression by the Communists against their own people. It gave the Americans a powerful new propaganda weapon against Communism.

 For twenty-eight years the Berlin Wall divided the city and prevented free movement between East and West Berlin. Its existence was a constant source of tension between NATO and the Warsaw Pact countries.

There were several confrontations between Soviet and American troops actually along the Wall. But America's refusal to back down caused the USSR to eventually give up the idea of taking over the whole city.

In June 1963 President Kennedy went to Berlin and saw for himself the Wall dividing the city. His visit underlined the US commitment to Berlin. Eventually, in 1989, as Communism in Europe disintegrated, the Berlin Wall was removed.

On 26 June 1963 President Kennedy peered over the Wall into a deserted looking Communist East Berlin

Today, in the world of freedom, the proudest boast is 'Ich bin ein Berliner.' There are many people in the world who really don't understand what is the great issue between the free world and the Communist world. Let them come to Berlin.

Freedom has many difficulties and democracy is not perfect, but we have never had to put a wall up to keep our people in... All free men, wherever they may live, are citizens of Berlin, and, therefore, as a free man, I take pride in the words 'Ich bin ein Berliner'.

President Kennedy speaking in West Berlin on 26 June 1963

4 What is meant by the term Cold War?
5 Why was President Kennedy so concerned about the USSR in Source C?
6 How useful is Source B in helping to explain the Cold War in 1962?
7 Explain why Berlin was so important to both sides in the Cold War.
8 In your own words explain how West Berliners might have felt when they heard Kennedy's words in Source D.

The Cuban missile crisis

Fidel Castro

The most serious crisis came in 1962 with the discovery that the USSR had secretly installed nuclear missiles in Communist-supported Cuba, a few miles from the coast of Florida. The USA was hostile to the revolutionary government of Cuba, led by Fidel Castro, after it nationalised many assets on the island that had previously belonged to Americans. For years the USA had supported the previous corrupt Batista regime and Cuba had been a popular holiday resort for Americans, with gambling and prostitution on a large scale. The US feared the spread of Communist influence in the Caribbean. The Soviets were happy to assist the new Cuban government. In 1961 an unsuccessful invasion by American-backed Cuban exiles at the Bay of Pigs underlined the threat to Castro from his powerful neighbour. Kennedy took the blame for the failure of this badly planned attack to remove Castro.

In October 1962 photographs taken by an American U-2 spy plane over Cuba revealed the presence of Soviet missile equipment. the USSR Premier, Nikita Khrushchev, felt justified in placing missiles in Cuba because of the possibility of an armed invasion by the USA of the island.

E

... we are firmly convinced that the USA will never resign itself to the existence of a socialist Cuba. We knew that they would do all they could to maintain the capitalist system in all the countries of the western hemisphere... the United States has reserved the 'right' to involve itself in the affairs of Europe, Asia, and the other continents, forming military alliances of imperialist countries to carry out a third world war...

To defend Cuba we proposed the installation of missiles. If North American imperialism had unleashed the invasion, no protest of ours would have stopped them. Only one thing could restrain them: the fear, the knowledge that if they began the invasion, the missiles would carry out their mission and the cities of North America would be left in ruins. We understood that placing such a weapon in Cuba was the most efficient way of defending it during that time.

Letter from the Soviet Premier, Nikita Khrushchev, to the Cuban Prime Minister, Fidel Castro, on 31 January 1963

F 'opposed to war'

This nation is opposed to war. We are also true to our word. Our unswerving objective, therefore, must be to prevent the use of these missiles against this or any other country, and to secure their withdrawal or elimination from the Western Hemisphere... We will not prematurely or unnecessarily risk the costs of world-wide nuclear war in which even the fruits of victory would be ashes in our mouth, but neither will we shrink from that risk at any time it must be faced.

Part of President Kennedy's televised address on 22 October 1962 to the people, telling them what action he was taking during the Cuban missile crisis

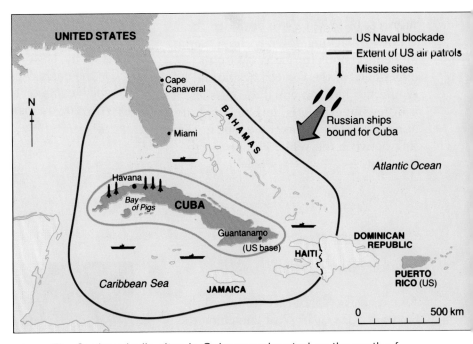

The Soviet missile sites in Cuba were located on the north of the island facing the coast of Florida, and were a direct threat to the USA

Kennedy had already been criticised by Republicans for failing to stop the Soviet military build up in Cuba. These were some of the options available to President Kennedy.

a Take no action and merely protest to Cuba and the USSR.
b Seek the assistance of the United Nations in which the USSR had the power to veto any action.
c Enforce a strict blockade of Cuba and stop any further missiles being installed.
d Invade Cuba and knock out the Soviet missiles.

The first option would have been taken as a sign of weakness, whilst the last could have led to a nuclear war. Not only Americans but people around the world waited anxiously to see what Kennedy would do in this, the most difficult crisis he had had to face. Many people including Dean Acheson, the Secretary of State, and the Joint Chiefs, who headed the armed forces, favoured an air strike, but the President decided to establish a blockade of Cuba. The problem was that if the USSR tried to break it then nuclear war could result, and if they did not remove the missiles then the possibility of an invasion and, consequently, war remained.

Khrushchev accused Kennedy of pushing mankind 'to the abyss of a world missile-nuclear war' and at first refused to back down, citing the presence of US missile sites in Turkey as further justification for Soviet ones in Cuba. Khrushchev said that Soviet captains would not obey American orders and tension rose as US warships began to stop and search ships on their way to Cuba. Neither the USSR nor the USA could afford the humiliation of retreat from the positions they had adopted in this, the most serious confrontation of the Cold War. In the end, the USSR did agree to withdraw the missiles, provided the USA promised not to infringe the sovereignty of Cuba. Khrushchev's concern was that 'if indeed war should break out, then it would not be in our power to stop it.' To the Americans it was a great victory and the popularity and prestige of President Kennedy rose enormously as the man who had stood firm against the USSR and won a great victory without any loss of life. For the Cubans, the whole crisis had been a disaster for it had worsened the enmity of the USA towards them and an economic blockade remained in force. In 1992 Castro criticised the USSR for backing down without gaining any concessions for Cuba, 'With the experience of the Soviets' hesitation, I would not have accepted the missiles.'

A few months later, in June 1963, it was agreed to set up a direct teletype hot-line link between the White House and the Kremlin.

9 Was it a good idea for the Soviets to site their missiles in Cuba?

10 Both the USA and USSR claimed victory in the crisis. Which side, if either, do you think came off best?

11 Why do you think the hot-line was set up?

'Space race'

An expensive 'space race' followed the Soviet success in 1957 of launching the first spacecraft. It proved the USSR could launch missiles against any point in the USA. American pride was hurt again in 1961 when the USSR launched the first man into space. President Kennedy was determined to achieve US predominance in space and, in 1962, NASA (National Aeronautics and Space Administration) launched John Glenn as the first man to orbit the Earth. Kennedy staked American prestige on a project to put a man on the Moon by the end of the 1960s. In 1969 America had a new hero in Neil Armstrong as he placed a US flag on the surface of the Moon. But the cost – $25,000 million – was huge. Although success in space demonstrated American superiority in technology and science, there were some people who complained that the money could have been put to better use in tackling problems on Earth.

12 To what extent was the 'space race' part of the Cold War?

13 Was the 'space race' a sensible use of resources?

 'That's one small step for man, one giant leap for mankind', said astronaut Neil Armstrong as he became the first human to step on the moon. The moon landing put the USA well ahead of the USSR in the 'space race'.

Assessments of President Kennedy

On 22 November 1963 the unimaginable occurred, when President Kennedy was assassinated whilst driving through Dallas in Texas. In spite of many investigations and a presidential commission, the Warren Commission, very few people believe that the alleged assassin, Lee Harvey Oswald, murdered the President on his own. Oswald was killed whilst in police custody and the reasons for the assassination remain one of history's greatest mysteries. For those old enough to be conscious of what had happened, the assassination was an unforgettably dreadful event that produced an enormous outpouring of grief.

Shortly after his death, 65% of voters claimed in an opinion poll that they had voted for Kennedy in 1960. A Gallup poll in 1976 showed that a majority of Americans regarded him as the greatest of all Presidents. The tragedy of his death makes dispassionate analysis difficult. A 1982 survey by the *Chicago Tribune* of forty-nine historians ranked Kennedy at fourteenth out of thirty-eight Presidents.

 This photograph, from an amateur film taken by Abraham Zapruder, shows Mrs Kennedy reaching out to a secret serviceman seconds after the President had been shot

 'America wept'

America wept tonight, not only for its dead young president, but for itself. The grief was general for somehow the worst in the nation had prevailed over the best... For something in the nation itself, some stain of madness and violence, had destroyed the highest symbol of law and order.

James 'Scotty' Reston, *New York Times*, 23 November 1963

Far from being a confrontationist, Kennedy was by temperament a conciliator... he had the capacity to refuse escalation – as he did ...in the Berlin crisis of 1961, in the Cuban missile crisis, and as surely would have done in Vietnam... If he had followed his own plan, he would have withdrawn American troops from Vietnam in 1965, instead of Americanizing the war that year as (President) Johnson did... Kennedy's commitment to politics as the greatest and most honourable adventure touched and formed a generation of young men and women in the 1960s. They were moved by his aspirations and shaped by his ideals.

Arthur Schlesinger, Jr., a distinguished historian and special assistant to President Kennedy, writing in 1986. He is convinced that Kennedy would not have embroiled the USA in the Vietnam War, but many others blame Kennedy for getting America involved in the first place.

▼ **A tragedy for the world**

To the world he will be remembered as the President who helped to bring the thaw in the Cold War. The real change came, however, only after Cuba. That crisis, taking the world to the edge of a nuclear war, left its mark on both him and Mr Khrushchev... He was not hopeful of an early improvement in relations. But he worked for such an improvement, as did Mr Khrushchev, and it came.

But he will be remembered as much as anything for his youth and friendliness... He was a true liberal, a thinker himself no less than a man of action.'

Extract from the leader, *The Guardian*, London, England, 23 November 1963

▼ **Bill Clinton and Kennedy in 1963**

While attending the American Legion Boys' Nation in 1963, fifteen year old Bill Clinton shook hands with President Kennedy at the White House, and came away believing that public service and politics was a noble career that he wished to follow. Thirty years later he became President. Clinton is one of those moved by Kennedy's 'aspirations and shaped by his ideals'. Allegations of marital infidelity have damaged the reputations of both Presidents.

The USA had a new President, former Vice President Lyndon Johnson, sworn in immediately after the assassination. The years of his presidency, until 1968, and those of his successor, Richard Nixon, were to be ones of great turbulence and strife as issues such as the Vietnam War, racism, abortion, drugs and student protest, divided Americans as never before. Bob Dylan, a very popular 1960s singer and songwriter, summed up what was happening to his country with his 1964 song 'The times they are a changing'.

14 How reliable and informative are Sources H and I.

15 Is there any evidence in this chapter to support Arthur Schlesinger's description of President Kennedy (Source H) as a 'conciliator'?

16 With reference to the sources and the text, explain why it has been difficult for historians to make an objective assessment of President Kennedy?

17 Did Kennedy's presidency live up to the title 'New Frontier'?

Essay:

i Using this chapter and pages 81 and 82, describe and assess the achievements of the Kennedy presidency.

ii Describe some of the problems that America faced in the early 1960s.

III How successful was Kennedy in his dealings with the USSR?

13 From civil rights to black power

In 1960 black or African-Americans, as they are generally called today, made up just over ten per cent of the population. In spite of some progress during the 1950s, the issue of their civil rights remained very important. Although President Kennedy felt no special commitment to the black civil rights movement, and was not keen to antagonise southern politicians, it was on this issue that his achievement was the greatest.

In the South, segregation remained in place. Segregation meant that black people were kept separate from whites. Southern politicians were determined to maintain segregation and to deny black people equal rights. This was in spite of court decisions and the policy of the federal government to end segregation. Most southern schools remained segregated. In five states there was not a single school which black and white pupils attended together. Intimidation of one kind or another prevented most black people in the South from registering to vote. Most public facilities, including lunch counters, libraries, and buses, remained strictly segregated. Such segregation was illegal but the law was not properly enforced in the South.

Black Americans were increasingly impatient at the lack of progress in obtaining their full civil rights. President Kennedy was accused of being too cautious and unwilling to upset the white southern politicians. The civil rights movement, which had started in the 1950s, gained strength.

Dr Martin Luther King mobilised thousands of blacks and whites in a massive campaign of non-violent civil disobedience and protest to demand desegregation of public facilities, including the right for blacks to attend all southern universities. In April 1963, whilst leading a demonstration in Birmingham, Alabama, King was arrested. The Chief of Police, Bull Connor, ordered his men to attack King's supporters with tear gas, fire hoses, dogs and even electric cattle prods. In all, more than 3,300 black men, women and children, who were peacefully demonstrating in support of their civil rights were hauled off to jail. Front page newspaper and TV pictures of police dogs ferociously attacking black people and fire hoses knocking them to the ground stirred public opinion. 'The civil rights movement,' said President Kennedy, 'should thank God for Bull Connor.'

A Black people registered to vote in the South

	1960	1966
Texas	35%	80%
Arkansas	37%	54%
Louisiana	30%	42%
Tennessee	52%	72%
Mississippi	5%	28%
Alabama	15%	49%
Virginia	24%	44%
North Carolina	31%	46%
South Carolina	16%	45%
Georgia	29%	43%
Florida	35%	62%

B

Letter from Birmingham City Jail

Part of a letter Martin Luther King wrote from jail in Birmingham, Alabama, in 1963 to explain why he thought mass demonstrations and protests were justified

We have waited for more than three hundred and forty years for our constitutional and God-given rights. The nations of Asia and Africa are moving with jet like speed toward the goal of political independence, and we still creep at horse and buggy pace toward the gaining of a cup of coffee at a lunch counter. I guess it is easy for those who have never felt the stinging darts of segregation to say, 'Wait.' But when you have seen vicious mobs lynch your mothers and fathers at will and drown your sisters and brothers at whim; when you have seen hate-filled policemen curse, kick, brutalize, and even kill your black brothers and sisters with impunity; when you see the vast majority of your twenty million Negro brothers smothering in an airtight cage of poverty in the midst of an affluent society; ... when you are humiliated day in and day out by nagging signs reading 'white' and 'coloured'... then you will understand why we find it difficult to wait.

'We shall overcome'

We shall overcome, we shall overcome,
we shall overcome some day.
Oh, deep in my heart I do believe,
that we shall overcome some day.

We'll walk hand in hand, we'll walk hand
  in hand,
we'll walk hand in hand, some day.
Oh, deep in my heart I do believe,
that we shall overcome some day.

We are not afraid, we are not afraid,
we are not afraid today.
Oh, deep in my heart I do believe
that we shall overcome some day.

This hymn became the anthem of the black civil rights movement. It has also been used by other protest groups.

An impressive demonstration of black unity and also white support was the March on Washington on 28 August 1963. More than 250,000 people, including 60,000 whites, marched through the capital to demand guaranteed civil rights for all. On the steps of the Lincoln Memorial, they heard Martin Luther King make an historic speech in which he repeated the words, 'I have a dream' over and over again as he described his hopes for racial harmony, and concluded with the moving optimism of the old spiritual song: 'Free at Last! Free at Last! Thank God Almighty, we are free at last.'

Spurred on by the protests and concerned at the continuing violence, and perhaps finally persuaded by his brother, Robert, who was the Attorney General, the top law officer, President Kennedy proposed new tough legislation saying that racial discrimination, 'has no place in American life or law'. But because of southern opposition, the new Civil Rights Act was not passed until after his death.

Great March on Washington DC, 28 August 1963. This was the largest march in the nation's history and demonstrated hope as well as determination by African-Americans to achieve their rights by the non-violent methods preached by Dr Martin Luther King.

▼ Anti-Discrimination Laws

1964 *Civil Rights Act* – outlawed racial discrimination in employment, in restaurants, hotels and amusement areas, and any bodies receiving government money including schools. The Equal Employment Opportunity Commission (EEOC) was set up to investigate complaints.
1965 *Voting Rights Act* – stopped racial discrimination with respect to the right to vote.
1967 Supreme Court ruled that state laws forbidding inter-racial marriages were unconstitutional.
1968 *Civil Rights Act* (Fair Housing Act) – made racial discrimination in housing illegal.

 President Johnson shakes hands with Dr Martin Luther King after signing the 1964 Civil Rights Act

1 How did segregation affect black Americans?
2 How serious a problem was it that so few black people could vote in 1960 (Source A)?
3 What is the main message of Dr King's words in Source B?
4 Dr King believed in non-violence. How might his words in Source B have been used to justify violence?
5 What do the words 'we shall overcome' in Source C mean?
6 How successful was Dr King's civil rights campaign 1960-64?

The demand for black power

Dr Martin Luther King preached non-violence. He wanted black people to be treated as equal citizens with whites. But there were other black leaders, such as Malcolm X, a black Muslim, who argued that King was too moderate and that militancy was necessary to confront white racism. King was concerned that their approach would lead to widespread bloodshed and be used by whites, including the President, as an excuse to turn against civil rights reforms. But for many young urban blacks Malcolm X's message was inspiring.

Malcolm X was a leader of the Nation of Islam. This Muslim organisation called for the total separation of black and white Americans. They showed their disgust at white America by replacing their second names, which they called 'slave names', with the letter 'X'.

E 'fight them and you'll get your freedom'

... I don't go along with any kind of non-violence unless everybody's going to be non-violent. If they make the Ku Klux Klan non-violent, I'll be non-violent, if they make the White Citizens' Council non-violent, I'll be non-violent. But as long as you've got somebody else not being non-violent, I don't want anybody coming to me talking any non-violent talk...

You get freedom by letting your enemy know that you'll do anything to get your freedom; then you'll get it. It's the only way you'll get it... fight them, and you'll get your freedom...

 Malcolm X

Malcolm X's advocacy of violence as a means of getting equal rights was very attractive to many young people. His parents had been murdered by the Ku Klux Klan and he too died violently when a black gunman assassinated him in 1965.

The civil rights movement had concentrated on trying to end segregation in the South. But there was also serious racial discrimination in the North. By 1965, 50% of blacks lived in the North. Most of them lived in city ghettos where there was slum housing, high unemployment and poor schools. Health care was inadequate. Public transport was poor which made it difficult for people to take jobs far from their home. The government of these cities, including the police, was in white hands. Wherever they lived, black Americans were far more likely to be poor than whites. In 1967 one third of all black families were living below the government's poverty level, compared with less than 10% of white families. The mortality rate for black babies was twice as high as for white babies.

 Family incomes in the 1960s
(Source: Bureau of the Census)

	(median income)	
	Black	**White**
1964	$5,921	$10,903
1965	$6,072	$11,333
1966	$6,850	$11,890
1967	$7,201	$12,162
1968	$7,603	$12,668

 'Black power'

I'm not going to beg the white man for anything I deserve – I'm going to take it we need power – we want black power.

Stokely Carmichael, a young militant black leader, in 1966

 Stokely Carmichael speaking in 1967

The slogan 'black power' became popular in 1966. It excited many black people with the idea that they should control their own communities. To many of them it meant the abandonment of Martin Luther King's non-violent protests. Groups such as the Black Panthers said blacks should defend themselves. Their members carried guns. The idea of black power also frightened many whites.

At the 1968 Olympic games, two US black athletes protested against racism in the USA by giving the black power salute during the awards ceremony. They also refused to look at the American flag.

7   What does 'black power' mean?
8   How would supporters of Dr King have reacted to 'black power'?
9   Explain why many young black people supported Malcolm X?

Black Panthers saluted a fallen comrade at his 1971 funeral. He was shot in the back during an alleged escape attempt from prison. The Panthers said that blacks should have their own armed self-defence or police forces to protect themselves from whites.

Riots against racism

During the mid 1960s a wave of riots took place in the ghettos of many major cities. In August 1965 the black ghetto in Watts, Los Angeles, erupted in violence. It was sparked off by white police officers roughly treating some blacks. Young men who attacked the police shouted 'This is the end of you, Whitey'. By the time the riot was over thirty-four people had been killed, hundreds injured, and four thousand people arrested. But whilst whites were horrified, to many blacks it was evidence that they would no longer be pushed around by whites. Other riots followed.

In 1967 came the worst riots in American history. Eighty-three people were shot dead. Most of them were black. Some people argued that the police used the riots as an excuse to attack black people. Large areas of cities such as Newark and Detroit were looted and burned. President Johnson was horrified and set up a national commission to find out the causes of the riots. According to their report, the riots 'involved Negroes acting against local symbols of white American society'. 'White racism', the report concluded, was chiefly responsible for the explosive mixture of poverty, discrimination and anger in the black community.

> Those buildings going up was a pretty sight. I sat right here and watched them go.
> And there wasn't nothing them honkies (whites) could do but sweat to put it out.'

The words of a Detroit rioter

Anger over police brutality and racism led to five days of rioting in Watts, a black section of Los Angeles

I

What white Americans have never fully understood – but what the Negro can never forget – is that white society is deeply implicated in the ghetto. White institutions created it, white institutions maintain it, and white society condones it.

It is time now to turn with all the purpose at our command to the major unfinished business of this nation. It is time to adopt strategies for action that will produce quick and visible progress. It is time to make good the promises of American democracy to all citizens – urban and rural, white and black, Spanish-surname, American Indian and every minority group.

National Advisory Commission on Civil Disorders, 1968

J A cleaning lady riots

I clean the white man's dirt all the time. When I got home and later when the trouble began, something happened to me. I went on the roof to see what was going on. Hearing the guns I felt like something was crawling on me, like the whole damn world was no good, and the little kids and the big ones and all of us was going to get killed because we don't know what to do. And I see the cops are white and I was crying. Dear God, I am crying! And I took this pop bottle and it was empty and I threw it down on the cops, and I was crying and laughing.

This woman in the black ghetto of Harlem in New York City, explained why she joined in the attack on the police

K Is violence necessary?
(Source: *Time* magazine, 6 April 1960)

	Can win rights without violence	violence probably necessary
Black opinion	%	%
1963	63	22
1966	59	21
1970	58	31
Age groups 1970		
14-21	55	40
22-29	58	31
30-49	55	33
50+	65	20

L Law and Order, 1970
(Source: *Time* magazine, 6 April 1970)

City	Blacks as a % of the population	Blacks as a % of the police force
Atlanta	38	10
Chicago	27	17
Detroit	39	5
Newark	40	10
Washington DC	63	21

Out of 300,000 lawyers only 3,000 are black.

The riots were a serious domestic crisis for the government. Whites tended to put the blame on black 'lawlessness' and demanded tougher action by the police and courts. Blacks, even those who did not take part, understood why black anger was boiling over.

The assassination of Martin Luther King

To the end of his life, Martin Luther King insisted on non-violence. Although other black leaders were more militant, King remained a controversial figure. He began to criticise the Vietnam War (Chapter 14). He made the connection between the huge sums of money spent on the war and the failure to tackle the poverty that so many black people suffered. 'We are spending all this money,' he said, 'for death and destruction, and not nearly enough for life and constructive development.' To the Federal Bureau of Investigation (FBI) King was a troublemaker. They targetted him. His private life was investigated and his phone conversations were tapped.

In 1968 King travelled to the southern city of Memphis in support of a strike by black refuse collectors. As he stood on the balcony of the Lorraine Motel he was shot dead by a man with a rifle from across the street. James Earl Ray was later arrested and imprisoned for King's murder. But many people believe that the killing was part of a large conspiracy.

Once again, riots broke out across America. Blacks were enraged by the murder of Dr King. To many of them it was 'white America that had murdered King'. It seemed to show that non-violence by blacks would be met by white violence. The manner of his death seemed to undermine the non-violence that Dr King had argued for all his life.

The funeral of Dr Martin Luther King

White backlash

What was the attitude of white Americans to black demands? Many whites seemed to blame blacks for their own situation. In 1969 a survey by *Newsweek* magazine claimed that 73% of whites agreed that blacks 'could have done something about slum conditions'. 55% thought that blacks were similarly to blame for their high rate of unemployment. Three quarters of white Americans were opposed to racially mixed schools. Riots and protests by blacks often provoked white anger. White voters demanded of their politicians that tough action be taken against black criminals.

 The blacks: too much, too soon

Do Negroes today have a better chance or worse chance than people like yourself?			
	Better	**Worse**	**Same**
To get well-paying jobs?	44%	21%	31%
To get a good education for their children?	41%	16%	41%
To get good housing at a reasonable cost?	35%	30%	27%
To get financial help from the government when they are out of work?	65%	4%	22%

(Survey of white opinion by *Newsweek* magazine, October 1969)

N Views of a 'briarhopper'

We do all the work. The niggers have got it made. They keep closing in and closing in, working their way into everything. Last three or four months you can't even turn on the damn TV without seeing a nigger. Us briarhoppers (transplanted southerners) ain't gonna stand for it. If a bunch of good ol' briarhopper Ku Kluxers had got a hold of Martin Luther King, he wouldn't have lived as long as he did.

Earnest Hayes, 58, a worker at the Armco steel plant in Ohio, quoted in *Newsweek*, 6 October 1969

By the end of the 1960s there was no going back for the black Americans. They took pride in themselves and in their African origins and culture. Whether whites liked it or not they were determined to pursue the goal of equality. Some progress had been made during the 1960s. The civil rights laws did lead to more integrated schools and far more black people voted in elections. In 1967 Carl Stokes was elected mayor of Cleveland, Ohio – the first black elected mayor of a major city. Other political successes followed. Gradually some black people were able to make the most of new opportunities available. Increasingly, large companies appointed blacks to senior positions. A black American, Colin Powell, became the chief general in the army. Even so, laws have not ended widespread racism. One third of American black families still struggle to survive below the poverty level compared with 10% of white families. The idea of equality in American society still remains distant for many of its citizens. Racial conflict remains a major problem in the 1990s and an important cause of much of the disharmony and violence in the USA.

O The position of African-Americans, 1960s-1990s
(Sources: Census Bureau; Dept. of Labor; EEOC)

Then			Now	
1963	10.8%	Unemployment	1993	13.8%
1965	280	Number of black elected officials	1993	7,552
1967	$4,325	Household income	1991	$18,807
1963	51%	Poverty rate	1991	32.7%
1964	25.7%	High school graduation rate	1991	38.7%
1965	8,854	Number of discrimination complaints	1992	49,000
1960	10.5%	Black Americans as percentage of the population	1990	12.1%

10 What clues are there in Sources H-L as to the causes of the riots?

11 What evidence is there that some people were pleased with the riots?

12 Describe the possible feelings of these people following the murder of Dr King:
(a) a supporter of Dr King
(b) a supporter of Malcolm X
(c) a white racist.

13 Do Sources M and N prove that white Americans were hostile to black demands?

14 Was violent protest ever justified?

15 With reference to chapters 4, 11, and 13, explain how some things have changed but others have stayed the same for black Americans.

Essay:
'I do not think white America is committed to granting equality to the American Negro ... this is a passionately racist country; it will continue to be so in the foreseeable future.' Using information throughout this book, discuss this opinion by Susan Sontag, a white American writing in the 1960s.

14 Defeat in Vietnam

America's longest war

The Vietnam War was America's longest war. It was also a costly defeat that caused deep divisions among Americans and damaged America's national pride. A great anti-war movement came into being which played an important part in ending the war. The anguish and arguments caused by the war have continued ever since. You will need to think about these questions as you study this topic:

- How did the USA become involved in a war in Vietnam which is nearly 9000 miles from the continental USA?
- Why did so many Americans turn against the war?
- What was fighting in Vietnam like for the thousands of young Americans sent there?
- Why did the USA find it so difficult to withdraw from Vietnam?
- Why was the militarily powerful USA defeated?
- What effect did defeat have on America's position in world affairs?

These questions remain unresolved in the minds of many Americans.

Timeline of US involvement in Vietnam

1954 Vietnam a divided country:
North Vietnam – Communist
South Vietnam – non-Communist

1956-60 US sends arms and millions of dollars to South Vietnam, fearing a takeover by the Communist North.

1961 President Kennedy orders first US military assistance to South Vietnam.

1964 North Vietnamese attack on US ships in Gulf of Tonkin. US military build-up increases.

1965 US Air Force starts bombing targets in North Vietnam.

1967 Anti-war demonstrations begin in the USA.

1968 Tet offensive shows the strength of the Vietcong.

1969 US fighting troops reach their maximum strength. Peace talks begin.

1970 US troops and planes attack Communist bases in Cambodia. National Guard soldiers kill four students at an anti-war demonstration in Ohio.

1972 North Vietnam invades South Vietnam. Most US troops withdrawn.

1973 US and North Vietnam sign a peace agreement. Last US troops leave.

1975 South Vietnam surrenders to North Vietnam and the country is reunited. Saigon, the South Vietnamese capital, renamed Ho Chi Minh City.

1977 President Carter pardons Vietnam-era draft evaders.

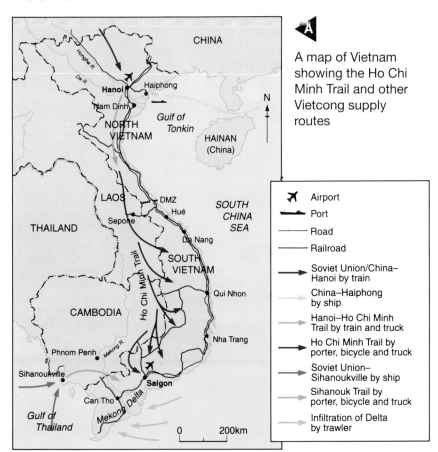

A map of Vietnam showing the Ho Chi Minh Trail and other Vietcong supply routes

✈	Airport
⚓	Port
—	Road
—	Railroad
→	Soviet Union/China–Hanoi by train
→	China–Haiphong by ship
→	Hanoi–Ho Chi Minh Trail by train and truck
→	Ho Chi Minh Trail by porter, bicycle and truck
→	Soviet Union–Sihanoukville by ship
→	Sihanouk Trail by porter, bicycle and truck
→	Infiltration of Delta by trawler

Americans go to Vietnam

Vietnam, in South East Asia, had been split by civil war. The Communists governed North Vietnam whilst the government in South Vietnam was strongly anti-Communist. But many South Vietnamese disliked their government for being corrupt and undemocratic. 50% of the land was owned by just 2% of the population. Although the main religion was Buddhism, the Roman Catholic Church was the single largest land-owner. The South Vietnamese government and the USA were seen as supporting these large and wealthy landowners. Not surprisingly, most South Vietnamese wanted a fairer spread of land ownership. They supported the Communist backed National Liberation Front (NLF) or Vietcong as the Americans called it. This grew into a large guerrilla army supplied along what was called the Ho Chi Minh Trail, with equipment from Russia and China as well as North Vietnam. During the late 1950s and early 1960 Vietnam was one of several Cold War trouble-spots. The USA did not want Communist North Vietnam to take over the South. Americans including Presidents Eisenhower and Kennedy supported the domino theory (see Source B). They attempted to support the South Vietnamese government, even though it was corrupt and undemocratic. US policy was to halt the spread of Communist power anywhere in the world. At the time of President Kennedy's death, there were 16,000 US soldiers in Vietnam. They were called 'advisers'.

 'Let every nation know'

> Let every nation know, whether it wishes us well or ill, that we shall pay any price, bear any burden, meet any hardship, support any friend, oppose any foe in order to assure the survival and success of liberty... In the long history of the world, only a few generations have been granted the role of defending freedom in its hour of maximum danger. I do not shrink from this responsibility I welcome it.

The words of President Kennedy in his inaugural address, January 1961

 President Kennedy and Vietnam in 1963 (1)

> In the final analysis, it is their war. They are the ones who have to win it or lose it. We can help them, we can give them equipment, we can send our men out there as advisers, but they have to win it, the people of Vietnam against the Communists.

President Kennedy in a TV interview, 3 September 1963

 The domino theory

In 1954, President Eisenhower warned: 'You have a row of dominoes set up and you knock over the first one and the last one will go over very quickly.' He feared that if Vietnam went Communist, neighbouring countries would fall just like a row of dominoes. Those countries carried on important trade with the USA.

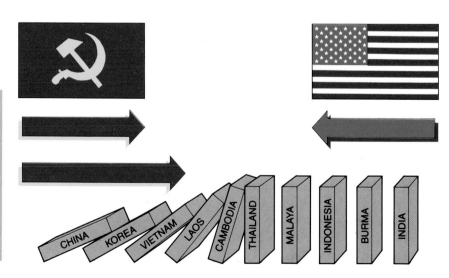

President Kennedy and Vietnam in 1963 (2)

At a meeting on October 5, 1963, the President considered the recommendation contained in the report of Secretary McNamara and General Taylor on their mission to South Vietnam.

The President approved the military recommendation contained in Section IB (1-3) of the report, but directed that no formal announcement be made of plans to withdraw 1,000 US military personnel by the end of 1963.

National Security Action Memorandum
No 204, The White House, 11 October 1963

1 Why was the government of South Vietnam unpopular with its own people?
2 Why was the USA concerned about what happened in South Vietnam?
3 What was the domino theory?
4 What kind of commitment did Kennedy make in Source C to countries such as South Vietnam?
5 Why do you think US soldiers in Vietnam in 1963 were called 'advisors'?
6 After studying Sources D and E, do you think Kennedy planned to involve the USA in an all-out war in Vietnam?
7 Can we believe the information in Sources D and E?

Johnson's war

By 1964 the South Vietnamese government was in serious danger of defeat by the Communists. The USA had two options. They could either withdraw their support or send in as many troops as were necessary. President Lyndon B Johnson, usually known quite simply as LBJ, decided to escalate the war. He had always been a firm believer in the domino theory. LBJ massively increased the number of American soldiers. Instead of being 'advisers' they were combat troops fighting alongside the South Vietnamese Army in an effort to defeat the Communists. LBJ's policy turned out to be quite disasterous. Why was Johnson so determined to achieve a military victory in Vietnam? How did he persuade Americans, including the US Congress, to support sending half a million soldiers to fight in Vietnam?

 US Forces in South Vietnam
(Source: Defense Department)

1962	9,000	(Kennedy Administration)
1963	15,000	"
1964	16,000	(Johnson Administration)
1965	60,000	"
1966	268,000	"
1967	449,000	"
1968	535,000	"
1969	539,000	(Nixon Administration)
1970	415,000	"
1971	239,000	"
1972	47,000	"

Note The average age of US soldiers in Vietnam was 19 years old, compared with an average of 26 years old in World War 2.

 LBJ's Position on Vietnam

We are there because we have a promise to keep... to leave Vietnam to its fate would shake the confidence of all these people in the value of American commitment.

If I left that war and let the Communists take over South Vietnam then I would be seen as a coward and my nation would be seen as an appeaser, and we would find it impossible to accomplish anything for anybody anywhere on the entire globe.

In August 1964, two American destroyers were attacked in the Gulf of Tonkin by North Vietnamese gunboats. Johnson called it an unprovoked act of war. In fact the destroyers had been assisting a South Vietnamese attack on North Vietnam. American anger over the attack on their ships led Congress to agree to the Tonkin Gulf Resolution. It gave the President the powers to mount an all-out war in Vietnam. There was no proper discussion as to whether or not America should go to war. After Tonkin, the civil war between the peoples of North and South Vietnam was 'Americanized'. One of Johnson's top advisers gave him this warning: 'Once on the tiger's back we cannot be sure of picking the place to dismount.'

The war in Vietnam

A massive US army was dispatched to Vietnam. Four years after Tonkin, as many as 543,000 US soldiers were fighting there. The cost in dead and wounded grew alarmingly. By the end of 1968 more than 30,000 Americans were dead. A further 100,000 had been wounded. In spite of all this the South Vietnamese and their US allies had been quite unable to defeat the Communists whose support became stronger.

To the Americans, the Vietnamese appeared to be poor and backward peasants. They lacked many of the sophisticated and powerful weapons that the USA as a superpower possessed. Why were the Americans, with all their military strength, unable to defeat the Vietcong and the North Vietnamese?

I wanna go to Vietnam
I wanna kill a Vietcong
With a knife or with a gun
Either way will be good fun

But if I die in the combat zone
Box me up and send me home
Fold my arms across my chest
Tell my folks I done my best

US Army marching song

 Fighting the Vietcong

He [the Vietcong] knows that he can't stand up to us in a fire fight due to our superior training, equipment and our vast arsenal of weapons. Yet he is able. Via his mines and booby traps, he can whittle our ranks down... In the month that I have been with the company, we have lost 4 killed and about 30 wounded. We have not seen a single verified dink [enemy soldier] the whole time, nor have we even shot a single round at anything.

US Lieutenant Robert Ransom in a letter to his parents told of the difficulty in getting to grips with the enemy. Shortly afterwards he was killed by a Vietcong mine.

A US personnel carrier in Vietnam. 'Dinks' and 'gooks' were insulting names that US soldiers called the Vietnamese. Often the Americans appeared to be racist towards the Vietnamese people.

J Cold War? Not for some

The Vietcong fought a guerrilla war in their own country. They were fighting on home ground and could easily blend in with the rest of the population. During the daytime they might appear to be ordinary peasants, whilst at night they would be laying mines to ambush American soldiers. All the time military equipment was brought from the North to all parts of the South by means of the Ho Chi Minh Trail. It was named after the great leader of North Vietnam, Ho Chi Minh, who inspired many Vietnamese to share his aim for a united Vietnam under a Communist government. The Vietcong, supported by many ordinary Vietnamese people, strongly believed in the cause they were fighting for. To them the Americans were a foreign invader. But the Vietcong could not have succeeded without considerable support from the Communist superpowers of the USSR and China. So the Cold War opponents, Russia and China versus the USA, confronted one another in what had started out as a civil war between the Vietnamese people.

Over half the Americans who died in combat were killed by small-arms fire. Most of the fighting was close combat by small units. The Vietcong perfected various ambush techniques. In addition, they constructed deadly booby traps. These were responsible for a further 11% of American deaths. There were mines, grenades, and sharpened bamboo 'pungi' stakes in camouflaged pits which terrified American troops.

US troops faced appalling conditions. There was the constant danger of ambush by the Vietcong. It is not surprising that American morale was often very low.

K Operation 'Junction City'

It was explained to us that anything alive in that area was supposed to be dead. We were told that if we saw a 'gook' [slang for Vietnamese] or thought we saw one, no matter how big or small, shoot first. No need for permission to fire. It was just an 'open turkey shoot'... men, women, and children, no matter what their ages all went into the body count. This operation went on for a few weeks. This was a regular 'search and destroy' mission in which we destroyed everything we found.

Sergeant James Weeks described orders he was given in May 1967

American military officers became frustrated that they could not beat their enemy. One general expressed some admiration when he reported, 'The ability of the Vietcong continuously to rebuild their units and to make good their loses is one of the mysteries of the guerrilla war.'

The Army used 'search and destroy' missions to hunt out Vietcong and their supporters. Entire villages were burnt to the ground if it was thought they had been used by the Vietcong. Men of military age were often killed. But sometimes if there was any resistance, other civilians were also killed. One of the worst incidents occurred at the village of My Lai. The villagers were rounded up and ordered into a ditch where they were shot to death by American soldiers. Between 450 and 500 men, women, and children died. Later, Lieutenant William Calley, was found guilty of ordering the massacre. But there were many other instances of innocent civilians being killed by American troops. Perhaps it is not surprising that this helped the Vietcong to win even more support among the South Vietnamese.

The US commenced the heavy bombing of North Vietnam. They hoped that by this they would be able to reduce the supplies being sent south and to force the North Vietnamese to seek a peace agreement. By the end of the war, seven million tons of bombs had been dropped on Vietnam. This was more than twice the total weight of bombs dropped in Europe and Asia in the Second World War. American planes also bombed areas in South Vietnam believed to be occupied by the Vietcong. Sometimes they dropped napalm, which burned everything it came into contact with. Crops, animals, homes and people were destroyed.

The war had become an American war. President Johnson and his military chiefs took all the military decisions. But although Johnson had escalated the war, he was unable to win it. The bombing appeared to strengthen the Communists' resolve to fight on. The Americans had badly under-estimated their determination. But Johnson would not end the war. 'I'm not, he said, 'going to be the first President to lose a war.'

US soldiers burning a Vietnamese village that had given support to the Vietcong. Actions like this turned more and more Vietnamese against the Americans.

L American doubts

I never thought it would go on like this. I didn't think these people had the capacity to fight this way. If I had thought they would take this punishment and fight this well and could enjoy fighting like this, I would have thought differently at the start.

Robert McNamara, US Secretary of Defense, made this comment to *Newsweek* magazine in late 1966

M Why did the US fail in Vietnam?

Because they were cocky, over-confident, sure of themselves, certain that they could win at a bearable cost, and that in the process they would turn back the Communist tide in Asia.

The view of American historian, Stephen Ambrose, 1976

The war devastated Vietnam. By 1970 at least 300,000 South Vietnamese civilians had been killed. Out of a population of 17 million, 5 million people were officially classed as refugees.

N Did the Vietnamese people matter?

> But I never sensed any concern (by President Johnson) for the other side. How many people were killed in the village? How many South Vietnamese, how many North Vietnamese, how many Vietcong? It was our lives, our country; and they didn't figure, those people.

This was how a top US official, Attorney General Ramsey Clark, recalled President Johnson's visits to the military situation room to find out about the progress of the war

8 What do you think Johnson meant by 'a promise to keep' in Source G?

9 What did the Americans think of the Vietnamese people?

10 How might the recipients of the letter, Source I, have felt?

11 Why were the Vietcong such good fighters?

12 Why did the USSR and China support the Vietcong?

13 What is your opinion of the orders outlined in Source K?

14 Were the Americans really fighting on behalf of the Vietnamese people?

15 Do Sources L and M support or contradict one another?

16 Does Source N prove that President Johnson did not care about the Vietnamese people?

17 A soldier has just returned from Vietnam and is telling another soldier who is about to be sent there about the war. Write down the discussion they might have had.

Opposition to the war

At first opposition to US involvement in Vietnam was quite small. Only two out of the 100 US Senators voted against the Tonkin Resolution. A 1964 opinion poll showed that 85% of Americans approved of Johnson's war policy. But as the casualties increased, and people saw the devastation and suffering in Vietnam on the TV news, criticism of the war increased. In October 1967, 35,000 anti-war demonstrators took part in a march in Washington DC. They shouted the slogan, 'Hey, hey LBJ, how many kids did you kill today?'. By 'kids' they meant not only Vietnamese children but also young US soldiers. In November 1969, more than 250,000 people staged a massive demonstration against the war. A 1969 poll showed that fewer than half of the American people were opposed to these anti-war protests. Americans were deeply divided over the war. On university campuses across the country there were demonstrations and strikes against the war. Many times protesters burned the US flag.

Older people who had served in the Second World War or fought against the Communists in Korea could not understand why so many young people were unwilling to support this war.

I WANT OUT

This anti-war poster is a parody of the Uncle Sam poster used in the First World War which is reproduced on page 8

 Americans ended up fighting each other over the war. Police and National Guardsmen often broke up anti-war protests with considerable violence.

 An anti-war statement

> We demand that no more American youth be sent to fight in a war that is helping neither them nor the Vietnamese people. We have learned lessons from Nazi Germany and will not go along with the aggressive war-making policies of any government, even if it happens to be our own.

Fifth Avenue Peace Parade Committee, 1967

 President Nixon calls protesters 'bums'

> You think of those kids out there [in Vietnam] They are the greatest. You see these bums blowing up the campuses ... they are the luckiest people in the world, going to the greatest universities and here they are burning up the books, I mean storming around about – get rid of the war. Out there [in Vietnam] we've got kids who are just doing their duty. They stand tall and they are proud.

President Nixon on 1 May 1970

Public opinion

> In view of the developments since we entered the fighting in Vietnam, do you think the United States made a mistake sending troops to fight in Vietnam?
>
> Yes   52%
> No   39%
> No opinion   9%

(Opinion poll conducted by Gallup in January 1969)

'Hell no, we won't go'

Some young Americans refused to go and fight. American men could be required to serve in the army. A system known as the 'draft' (Selective Service System) selected those who had to join up. 'Draft dodging' became widespread. Protesters publicly burned their draft cards. Many simply went into hiding. By 1968 about 10,000 of them had moved out of the USA into Canada. Others travelled to live in Sweden and a few to England. At the time it

seemed it might be a permanent exile. In 1977 President Jimmy Carter granted a pardon so that they could return to the USA.

Around the world public opinion turned against the Americans. Massive and sometimes violent demonstrations against American policy took place in many world capitals, including outside the US Embassy in London. To the demonstrators it was a David against Goliath struggle.

 Millions of young people joined the peace movement. Bitter arguments over the war went on in many homes.

R A refusal to fight

I am enclosing the order for me to report to my pre-induction physical exam for the armed forces. I have absolutely no intention to report for that exam, or for induction, or to aid in any way the American war effort against the people of Vietnam.

Written by a student in May 1968. He was sentenced to four years in prison for his refusal to serve in the army.

The killings at Kent State University

The most serious incident in the anti-war protests occurred on 4 May 1970. Universities had exploded in angry protest after President Nixon extended the war by attacking Vietnam's neighbour, Cambodia. At Kent State University, Ohio, hundreds of students threw stones and jeered at National Guardsmen (soldiers) sent in to keep order. Without warning the troops fired a volley of shots that left four defenceless students dead and a further nine wounded. Twenty-eight soldiers had fired sixty-one bullets.

People could not believe that such violence had occurred at a university. Students at four hundred and fifty colleges and universities immediately went on strike. The father of one of the dead students, nineteen year old Alison Krause, made the emotional comment, 'My child was not a bum.' But the violence had not ended. A few days later two students at another university who were protesting against the killings at Kent State were shot dead by police. These killings were a turning point in the war. In the words of one historian, 'the blood spilled at Kent gave the war in Vietnam the dark stain of civil war and, in time, made it insupportable.'

 The violence of war reached America. National Guardsmen fired tear gas at protesting students at Kent State University. Minutes later they shot four students dead. The tragedy at Kent State was the most serious incident in the anti-war protests.

T A father's anger

She resented being called a bum because she disagreed with someone else's opinion. She felt that our crossing into Cambodia was wrong. Is this dissent a crime? Is this a reason for killing her? Have we come to such a state in this country that a young girl has to be shot because she disagrees deeply with the action of her government?

Arthur Krause talking about his daughter on TV, 5 May 1970

U

These few days after Kent State were among the darkest of my presidency. I felt utterly dejected when I read that the father of one of the dead girls had told a reporter, 'My child was not a bum.

Richard Nixon in his memoirs, 1978

Black Americans and the war

Some of the first opposition to the Vietnam War came out of the Black American civil rights movement. Muhammad Ali, the heavyweight boxing champion of the world, was stripped of his title after he refused to serve in what he called a 'white man's war'. Black leaders such as Martin Luther King complained that money spent on the war should instead be spent on relieving poverty in American cities. In the end, $141 billion was spent on the war, whilst spending on schools, health care and public housing was cut back. King criticised the government for sending poor black Americans to fight and kill poor Vietnamese.

V Dr Martin Luther King speaks out

We were taking the young Black men who had been crippled by our society and sending them 8000 miles away to guarantee liberties in Southeast Asia which they had not found in Southwest Georgia and East Harlem. So we have been repeatedly faced with the cruel irony of watching Negro and White boys on TV screens as they kill and die together for a nation that has been unable to seat them together in the same schools. So we watch them in brutal solidarity burning the huts of a poor village.

Martin Luther King speaking in 1967

W Black protest against the draft

No Mississippi Negroes should be fighting in Vietnam for the White man's freedom, until all the Negro people are free in Mississippi.
Negro boys should not honour the draft.

Protest leaflet by young Black Americans in 1965, after their classmate had been killed in Vietnam

18 Why did opposition to the war grow?
19 Were the writers of Sources O and R disloyal to their country?
20 Why did so many young people oppose the war?
21 How might a veteran of the Second World War have tried to persuade the writer of Source R that he should change his mind?
22 Was it right to send the writer of Source R to prison?
23 How do you think people reacted to Sources S and T?
24 What is the link between Sources P and U?
25 Why were the killings at Kent State a 'turning point in the Vietnam War'?
26 Why was Dr King so angry about the Vietnam War (Source V)?
27 The Vietnam War was the first time that large numbers of Americans had opposed their country going to war. Why was the anti-war movement so strong?

How did America withdraw from Vietnam?

In 1968, when it was clear that there was to be no easy victory, President Johnson decided not to stand for re-election as President. Members of his own Democratic Party criticised him for getting the country into such a difficult and costly war. Instead, Richard Nixon, a Republican, was elected on the promise to bring 'peace with honour'.

> Give us six months, and if we haven't ended the war by then, you can come back and tear down the White House fence.

Henry Kissinger, President Nixon's chief adviser, to a group of anti-war Quakers in 1968

> Let me speak to you honestly, frankly, open heartedly. You are a liar.

North Vietnamese official, Le Duc Tho to Henry Kissinger, 1970

Nixon's first plan was to gradually reduce American forces in Vietnam but increase military support to the South Vietnamese Army. This was called 'Vietnamization'. All it did was to continue the fighting. Nixon, like Johnson, did not want to be the first President to lose a war.

▼ Nixon's View

> For the United States the first defeat of our nation's history would result in a collapse of confidence in American leadership not only in Asia but throughout the world.

President Nixon in 1969

But Nixon did open peace talks with the North Vietnamese. These took place in Paris. Finally, in January 1973 the USA signed an 'agreement on ending the war and restoring peace in Vietnam'. A ceasefire between North and South Vietnam was established. The USA promised to withdraw its troops. They also promised to respond 'with full force' to any attack by the North on the South. A few weeks later the last combat troops returned to America.

In 1972 the Congress passed a new law, the *War Powers Act*. It compels the President to justify sending soldiers into any war within thirty days. After that time, Congress has to approve of any further military action.

In 1975 the North Vietnamese launched a massive invasion of the South. The USA refused to help them and the South Vietnamese government were quickly defeated. Vietnam became a single nation under a Communist government.

There was chaos as the last Americans fled from Saigon in April 1975, as the Communists took control of all South Vietnam. US policy in South Vietnam had completely failed.

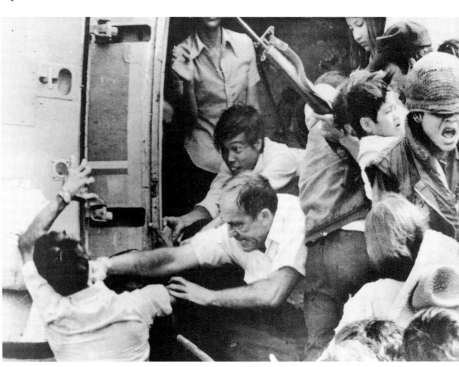

The war was over. Americans, however, found it difficult to put it behind them. It was the nation's first ever military defeat. The names of each of the 58,156 Americans killed are inscribed on a huge memorial in Washington DC. Vietnam Vets, as ex-soldiers who fought in the war are known, keep vigil there. It is a place of great emotion. The Vietnam War remains the most controversial and tragic episode in twentieth-century American history.

28 Was Le Duc Tho right when he said Kissinger was a liar?
29 Why did it take so long for the US to withdraw its troops from Vietnam?
30 Do you think the US achieved 'peace with honour'?
31 Was the Vietnam War a 'disaster' for the USA?

Essays:

i) President Nixon said: 'The North Vietnamese cannot defeat or humiliate the USA. Only Americans can do that.' What do you think he meant and was he right?

ii) Why did Americans think in 1965 that they could win in Vietnam? What changed their minds?

▼ The lessons of Vietnam

Today, Americans still disagree on the main issues and lessons of the war. Some believe US participation was necessary and just. Many of these people say the war was lost because the United States did not use its full military power and because opposition at home weakened the war effort. But other Americans believe US involvement was immoral and unwise. Some of them feel US leaders stubbornly made the war a test of the nation's power and leadership. Others view the conflict as a civil war that had no importance to US security. Since Vietnam, many Americans have argued that the nation should stay out of wars that do not directly threaten its safety or vital interests.

American historian George Herring writing in 1988

The Vietnam War Memorial is a constant reminder of all the Americans who were killed in the Vietnam War. As well as all those who died, 300,000 others were wounded, of whom almost 100,000 returned without one or more limbs. Americans have found it difficult to 'put Vietnam behind them'.

15 *A* divided nation

The failure of the 'Great Society'

President Lyndon B Johnson, LBJ, was a decent man. He became President following the assassination of President Kennedy. Johnson wanted to build on President Kennedy's policies and he had far-reaching ideas to tackle problems of unemployment, bad housing, and inadequate medical care. Johnson declared 'a war on poverty'. He called his policies the 'Great Society'. Johnson won the 1964 election by a large majority. But four years later he decided not to stand for a second term of office, although he was entitled to. By then members of his own Democratic Party were organising against him. Johnson left office a disappointed man. He had not achieved as much as he had hoped. He had also taken the USA into a full-blown and disasterous war in Vietnam (see Chapter 14)

Americans were divided over many of these issues. Many of them believed that there were many opportunities to get work and to do well and that the poor were responsible for their own problems. On the other hand, many people in the cities demanded more action. Opposition to the Vietnam war grew. Violent demonstrations and race riots were commonplace. During the last year of Johnson's presidency, two political assassinations shocked the nation. The leading black campaigner, Dr Martin Luther King, was shot dead. Senator Robert Kennedy, the brother of President Kennedy, was murdered as he campaigned for the presidency. Americans were frustrated and angry. Most of all, they felt a sense of despair at their government's failure to sort out the problems.

▼ A The Great Society

I want to be the President who educated young children to the wonders of their world… who helped to feed the hungry and to prepare them to be taxpayers instead of tax-eaters… who helped the poor to find their own way and who protected the right of every citizen to vote in every election… who helped to end hatred among his fellow men and who promoted love among the people of all races and all regions and all parties… who helped to end war among the brothers of this earth.

President Johnson in a speech, 1965

What did President Johnson accomplish?

- War on Poverty
  The Economic Opportunity Act, 1964, provided training to disadvantaged youths aged 16-21; helped low-income students to work their way through college; recruited volunteers to work and teach in low income slum areas.

- Medicare and Medicaid, 1965
  This provided medical insurance for the over 65s and hospital care for the poor.

- Environmental protection
  A series of laws aimed to ensure clean water and enforce air quality standards.

- City improvements
  The Development Act, 1964, provided money for replacing inner city slums with new homes.

- Highway safety
  Compulsory safety standards for cars and a national highway safety programme.

In addition, President Johnson took important steps to improve the civil rights of black Americans (Chapter 13). But these well-intended actions did not solve the problems of poverty and disadvantage. They did, however, raise people's hopes and increased their frustrations. In the inner city slums, people's protests frequently turned violent. Anger over the Vietnam War added to the protests in an increasingly divided nation. Republicans criticised Johnson for spending money on welfare. Some Democrats criticised him for failing to solve problems and for the war.

Views on President Johnson

 B **Johnson criticised**

The inspiration and commitment of the Great Society have disappeared. In concrete terms, the President simply cannot think about implementing the Great Society at home while he is supervising bombing missions over North Vietnam. There is a kind of madness in the assumption that we can raise the many billions of dollars necessary to rebuild our schools and cities and public transport and eliminate the pollution of air and water while also spending tens of billions to finance an 'open-ended war in Asia'

Democratic Senator J William Fulbright, 1966

 C **Johnson's decline**

The overriding cause for Lyndon Johnson's decline from the peaks of 1964 and 1965 is the war in Vietnam – too confidently entered upon, too little understood, to costly... Lyndon Johnson came into office seeking a Great Society in America and found instead an ugly little war that consumed him.

Comment in the *New York Times*, 1 April 1968, the day after Johnson announced he would not seek re-election

1 What did President Johnson mean by the 'Great Society'?
2 What reasons do Sources B and C give for Johnson's failure?

'Make love not war' – The youth revolt

During the second half of the 1960s many young people turned against the lifestyles of their parents. Some of them turned to radical politics as well. Their behaviour challenged the established values of older people. Parents found it difficult to understand or tolerate the behaviour of their children. Hippie clothes, with long hair and mystical religions, became fashionable, along with the use of drugs and permissive sexual behaviour. 'Make love not war' was their slogan. Many of them were middle class white college students. They were angry over the war in Vietnam, and racism, and also rejected the idea of getting a good well paid job. They had no faith in established politicians. True hippies were entirely non-violent. Because they often wore flowers and handed them out to the police, they were called 'flower children' and often settled in communes. San Francisco became the hippie capital of America. Their behaviour, in particular their use of drugs, frequently brought them into confrontation with the police. As *Newsweek* magazine reported in 1969, 'To the students, most policemen have become 'pigs', brutal representatives of an uptight power structure'.

 A 'flower child'. Parents were usually horrified if their children became hippies.

Music was an important part of this youthful rebellion. The British invasion by pop groups including the Beatles and the Rolling Stones changed the pop music scene. The songs were about peace, free love, and drugs. Huge outdoor rock festivals attracted thousands of hippies. The largest was at Woodstock in 1969. It became an enduring symbol of the hippie lifestyle. About half a million young people turned up to hear the music, use cheap marijuana, and swim nude in the lake. Artists including Jimi Hendrix, Janis Joplin, and Joan Baez, sang about sex, drugs, and opposition to the Vietnam War. Parents, teachers, and politicians were generally appalled by this behaviour.

Starting in 1965, a wave of demonstrations and strikes affected nearly every university and college. Students demanded more say in their own education. They wanted to take part in running the universities. They wanted an end to many of the college rules and restrictions imposed on them. Because most colleges had military cadets and training, there were often violent clashes over the Vietnam War. Students for a Democratic Society (SDS) became a powerful movement that spoke for student idealism. Police and college authorities tried to stop SDS so-called 'outside agitators' visiting their campuses. Parents and politicians reacted with fury, accusing students of being ungrateful for the benefits American society gave them. Police and even soldiers were used to break up protests.

D The fate of the 'flower children'

Many of the flower children themselves grew tired of their riches-to-rags existence and returned to school to become lawyers, doctors, politicians, and accountants. The search on the part of alienated youth for a better society and a good life was strewn with both comic and tragic aspects, and it reflected the deep social ills that had been allowed to fester throughout the post-World War II period.

Historians George Brown Tindall and David Shi in America, 1992

▼ Janis Joplin was a popular hippy rock star. Tragically, she died in 1970 at the age of only 27 from a heroin overdose.

3 Why did teachers and parents criticise the hippie lifestyle?
4 What arguments might a parent have used to stop their 16 year old son or daughter attending the Woodstock Festival?
5 What advantage does a secondary source such as Source D have over a primary source?

The Woodstock Festival was described as a 'coming together for rock, drugs, sex and peace'. It was the high point of the hippie culture.

The women's movement

During the 1950s most women as well as men seemed to accept that a woman's place was in the home (see page 66). The 1960s saw the emergence of a new feminism that took much of its inspiration and some of its tactics from the civil rights movement.

The women's movement was launched in 1963 by a very influential book, *The Feminine Mystique* by Betty Friedan. She argued that most women were not content as housewives, and made the sensational claim that the American middle-class home had become 'a comfortable concentration camp' for women. The book became a bestseller. People began to speak of 'Women's Liberation'. In 1966 Friedan and other women set up the National Organization for Women (NOW).

Demonstrations like this one by women were frequently shown on TV news programmes

Betty Friedan helped make women aware of the importance of feminism in their lives

E Wages: men and women, 1965*
(Source: US Department of Labor)

	Men	**Women**
Factory workers	$5,752	$3,282
Service industries	$4,886	$2,784
Sales staff	$7,083	$3,003
Clerical	$6,220	$4,237
Professional	$8,233	$5,573
Managers, executives	$8,658	$4,516

*Median wages per year

F NOW Bill of Rights

1. Equal Rights Constitutional Amendment
2. Enforce Law Banning Sex Discrimination in Employment
3. Maternity Leave Rights in Employment and Social Security Benefits
4. Tax Deduction for Home and Child Care Expenses for Working Parents
5. Child Day Care Centres
6. Equal and Unsegregated Education
7. Equal Job Training Opportunities and Allowances for Women in Poverty
8. The Right of Women to Control Their Reproductive Lives.

Adopted at NOW's first national conference, Washington DC, 1967

Feminists used petitions, strikes, and legal action to push employers to increase wages and open top level jobs to women. At the same time, women were encouraged to protest against male sexism. Women invaded all-male bars and clubs, burned men's magazines that they said exploited women and also the traditional women's magazines with articles on cooking and beauty. Married women were urged to keep their own surnames. One of the most publicised protests took place against the annual beauty contest, the Miss America Pageant. Feminists claimed it insulted women. Many men ridiculed these and other campaigns. Hugh Hefner, publisher of the successful men's magazine *Playboy*, told his staff; 'These chicks are our natural enemy. It's time to do battle with them. They are inalterably opposed to the romantic boy-girl society *Playboy* promotes'.

What did the 'Women's Liberation' movement achieve?

In the early 1970s the highly publicised protests faded away. However, there is no doubt that women were far more conscious of their rights. Many working class women had no time for some of the feminist campaigns, but they did support the demand for equal pay. Most people were aware that sexual discrimination was widespread and many now considered it to be wrong.

Employment discrimination in government jobs was ended. In 1972, colleges were required to ensure equal educational opportunities for women. Increasingly more and more women have pursued careers and by the 1990s far more women than ever before hold important positions in every profession, including politics. The social changes which started noisily in 1965 became, during the 1970s and 1980s, a quiet revolution.

7 What do the demands in Source F tell us about the treatment of women in the 1960s?

8 How would people have reacted to the differences in wages described in Source E?

9 Why were feminists sometimes made fun of?

10 Write a letter to Hugh Hefner in support of the Women's Liberation Movement.

'Red power'

The first North Americans were the Native American Indians. They had suffered dreadfully during the nineteenth century at the hands of the US Government. They were driven off the land they had used for centuries and confined on reservations. In the process, hundreds of thousands were annihilated, and whites did everything they could to destroy the traditional Native American way of life. Their numbers dwindled from well over a million to 237,000 in 1900, and it seemed possible they might disappear altogether.

Some Native Americans refused to knuckle down and allow their culture to be destroyed by the whites.

 Native American population, 1900-1980
(Source: Bureau of the Census)

1900	237000
1910	277000
1920	244000
1930	343000
1940	345000
1950	357000
1960	524000
1970	793000
1980	1,364000

Of all the minority groups, the Native Americans were by far the worst off. Many of them still lived on reservations where they missed out almost entirely on the nation's growing prosperity. Native American unemployment was ten times higher than other Americans. On average they lived twenty years less than everyone else. Most tragic of all was that the suicide rate for Native American Indians was one hundred times higher than for whites.

As the civil rights and other protest movements developed during the 1960s, Native American Indians began to organise their own campaign to improve their lives. They wanted to correct many of the injustices their people had suffered. In 1968 the American Indian Movement (AIM) was set up. It's slogan was 'red power'. They directed their attacks against the government who had, they said, broken all of the four hundred treaties they had made with the Indian Nations. AIM argued that the government had illegally taken their lands. The trouble was that these lands were now lived on by millions of Americans. Other lands were exploited by oil and mineral companies.

H 'We'll right the wrongs'

The Pilgrims had hardly explored the shores of Cape Cod four days before they had robbed the graves of my ancestors, and stolen their corn, wheat, and beans...
Our spirit refuses to die. Yesterday we walked the woodland paths and sandy trails. Today we must walk the macadam highways and roads. We are uniting. We're standing not in our wigwams but in your concrete tent. We stand tall and proud and before too many moons pass we'll right the wrongs we have allowed to happen to us.

This speech by a Native American was banned from the 1970 annual celebration of the landing of the Pilgrim Fathers

Through the courts AIM won significant settlements. Of course the government would not give them the land, but, instead, they were awarded huge financial sums. In some cases the Indians said they didn't want the money. It was the land, taken from them by force in the last century, that they wanted back. The Supreme Court awarded the Lakota Sioux tribe $105 million for the theft of the Black Hills in South Dakota. They rejected the award and continue to insist on the return of their land.

Oglala Sioux tribesmen guarding Wounded Knee during their occupation of the historic site

In March 1973 several hundred Native American Indians occupied Wounded Knee in South Dakota and declared it 'liberated territory'. It was the site of a brutal massacre of nearly two hundred Indians by the US Army in 1890. Among local Indians unemployment was over 53%. Their life expectancy was just forty-six years. The protesters presented the government with a list of grievances that included broken treaties and bad treatment by the local police. Two hundred FBI officers and other police surrounded Wounded Knee. The siege lasted seventy-one days and aroused interest all over the USA and the world. There was a great deal of public support for the Native American Indians' cause.

By the time it was over, two Indians had been killed by the police, many arrests were made and the village of Wounded Knee burnt down. But the government did agree to study the Indians' grievances. Wounded Knee remains a symbol of Native American Indian defiance and demand for equal treatment with all other Americans.

11 What evidence would be useful to explain the condition of the Indians in the 1960s and 1970s?
12 What does the term 'red power' mean?
13 Why did the Indians become more militant in the later 1960s?

Urban unrest: A nation of violence?

Violent protests, riots, and political assassinations all gave the impression, both to Americans and the rest of the world, that America was a very violent society. As well as news coverage, TV programmes and films often boosted this impression. People were afraid to go outside their homes. One senior lawyer made the comment, 'fear of random attack imprisons us as surely as any Berlin Wall'.

Increasingly it was the inner cities where the problems were the greatest. Those who could afford it, especially the middle classes, fled from the cities to new suburban communities.

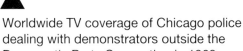
Worldwide TV coverage of Chicago police dealing with demonstrators outside the Democratic Party Convention in 1968 seemed to confirm the view that America was a very violent country

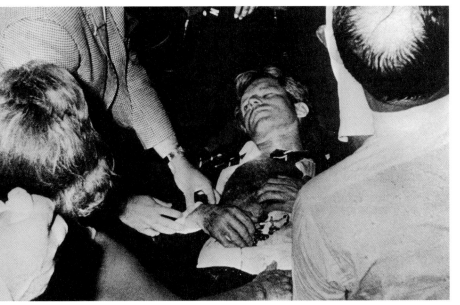

The 1968 assassination of Bobby Kennedy, President Kennedy's brother, caused a wave of anger and despair. Assassination seemed to have become a part of the political process.

It was a trend that had started in the 1950s but during the 1960s the process speeded up. Many downtown businesses closed down as new large shopping malls were built around the edges of towns and cities. This 'urban flight' left mainly the poor living in the cities. They paid little in taxes and so city councils lacked funds for new homes and schools. Crime flourished in these deprived communities and that made it even more difficult to attract investment and jobs to the inner cities.

A great deal of the crime involved the use of guns. In the 1960s there were more than fifty million guns in private hands and it was clear that there was a strong case for tough gun control laws. However, the second amendment of the US Constitution guarantees that, 'The right of the people to bear arms shall not be infringed'. That amendment was agreed in 1791 when armed civilians were needed to protect the country. In the 1960s a powerful gun lobby, led by the National Rifle Association (NRA), used this amendment to support their argument that all citizens should be allowed to keep a gun. It was claimed that law-abiding citizens needed guns to protect themselves from rioters and criminals. Some communities organised vigilante groups to protect their homes and businesses.

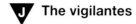

J The vigilantes

Vigilantes take the form of night patrols. They mean to make the streets safe... in some small towns they tote guns, and in others they are sufficiently in league with the police to ride around in police cars. In one place their targets are robbers or muggers, in another Negroes or radicals or homosexuals. It is a small and ugly symptom. It would be a tragic thing for America if the middle class, the silent majority, provoked by some appalling wave of rioting and violence, found its voice and used it not to preach but to improvise law and order.

Alastair Cooke, Letter from America, BBC Radio 4, 19 October 1969

Middle class Americans were often called 'the silent majority'. They were dismayed by what was happening to their country. They voted for Richard Nixon, a conservative Republican, who took office as President in 1969. He had served under Eisenhower as Vice President in the 1950s. People wanted a return to the stability and prosperity of those years.

14 Why were people so concerned about violence in 1968?
15 What is the danger that is worrying Alastair Cooke in Source J?
16 Which of Sources I and J is fact and which opinion and why?
17 Who were the 'silent majority'?
Essay: Does the term 'divided nation' accurately describe the USA during the 1960s?

I Crime explosion, 1960-1968

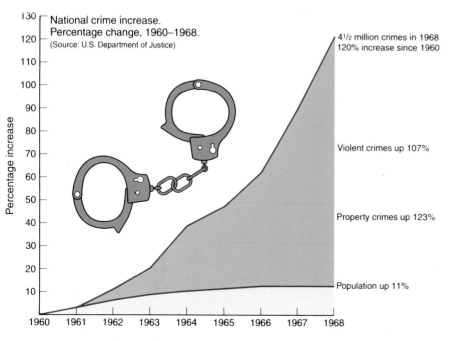

National crime increase. Percentage change, 1960–1968. (Source: U.S. Department of Justice)

4½ million crimes in 1968 120% increase since 1960

Violent crimes up 107%

Property crimes up 123%

Population up 11%

16 From Cold War to détente

During President Kennedy's Administration (1961-63) the USA and the USSR had stood on the brink of nuclear war over Berlin and Cuba (Chapter 12). There was the constant danger that the Cold War which had lasted since 1945 would lead to a nuclear third world war. Each side continued to blame each other for the tension. The USA feared the USSR's ambition to extend their power and influence over more and more of the world. On the other hand, the USSR was concerned that America was determined to destroy their Communist system. In addition, a second great Communist power, China, became increasingly important and militarily powerful. But China disagreed with the USSR over how best to run a Communist system. China shared a long border with the USSR. Their increasing hostility towards one another during the 1960s and 1970s was also a threat to peace. China did not have nuclear weapons but its huge army was a potential danger to countries in Asia that were supported by the USA.

In spite of all this and the continuing Vietnam War (Chapter 14), the years 1963-78 saw a gradual reduction in tension. Several important top level meetings and weapons treaties between the USA and USSR helped to reduce the threat of war. Eventually confrontation between East (USSR and the Warsaw Pact) and West (USA and NATO) was replaced by détente. Détente is a French word that means a 'relaxation of tension'. The relations between the two Superpowers improved considerably.

A Military balance sheet, 1974

Among Three Major Powers. . .

MILITARY BALANCE SHEET

TROOP STRENGTH (active-duty forces)	
U.S.A.	2,100,000
U.S.S.R.	4,200,000
CHINA	3,000,000

INTERCONTINENTAL MISSILES	
U.S.A.	1,054
U.S.S.R.	1,590
CHINA	0

SUBMARINE-LAUNCHED MISSILES	
U.S.A.	656
U.S.S.R.	700
CHINA	0

STRATEGIC BOMBERS	
U.S.A.	498
U.S.S.R.	160
CHINA	0

Source: U.S. Dept. of Defense

Nixon and détente

Richard Nixon hated Communism. Since 1946 he had built his political reputation by taking a tough stand against Communism and against those politicians, especially Democrats, who he thought were 'soft' on Communism. Yet as President (1969-74) it was Nixon who achieved the friendliest relations between the USA and both the USSR and China since the start of the Cold War. Because no one could ever accuse Nixon of being sympathetic to the Communists, he was able to reach compromise agreements with them. This thaw in the Cold War was President Nixon's greatest achievement.

By mid 1971, President Nixon was eager to end the Cold War. For several years it had been clear that the USA would not win a nuclear war. There would be no winner. US military forces could not defend the country, they could only retaliate. USSR armed forces were in exactly the same position. In a nuclear war both sides, and the rest of the world as well, would have been devastated. The Russians and the Chinese wanted friendlier relations with the USA. Americans, tired and fearful of the Cold War, and in despair over Vietnam, were in the mood to pursue peace even if it meant making compromises with the Communists.

 B Nixon on Communism, 1961

> The Communist threat is total. And so must be the arsenal of weapons we must have at our disposal to meet it... Mr Khrushchev [USSR leader] and his colleagues are fighting the battle for the world with all weapons – military, economic, political, propaganda... we must do the same if we are going to battle them on equal terms.'

Richard Nixon in his book *Six Crises*, 1961

C Nixon on Communism, 1968

> To the leaders of the Communist world, we say: After an era of confrontation, the time has come for an era of negotiation... we extend the hand of friendship to the Russian people, and to the Chinese people.

Richard Nixon in a speech in 1968

Diplomatic revolution

In 1970 President Nixon announced a new style of policy in dealing with the Communist countries. This new approach, Nixon said, 'shows a very significant shift from those policies of the past to the new policies dealing with the world as it is today.' Instead of continual military and other threats against the USSR and China, Nixon was proposing that they should all learn to get along with one another instead of constantly threatening to destroy each other's political system. The policy was mainly the idea of Nixon's main foreign policy adviser, Dr Henry Kissinger. It was called a 'diplomatic revolution'. Diplomats, officials representing their countries, travelled between Washington, Moscow and Beijing, to bring about closer and friendlier relations.

Nixon's aims were to:
  (i) discourage Russian and Chinese expansion
  (ii) limit the costly arms race
  (iii) reduce Russian and Chinese support for Third World countries.

But if these were the American intentions then why did the Russians and Chinese co-operate? Both China and the USSR had various internal problems. They needed to boost their economies and produce more consumer goods to satisfy their own people. The burden of heavy military expenditure was difficult to bear. There was also serious tension between China and Russia. During the 1960s they came to both hate and fear one another. There were serious incidents along their border. Both of these Communist countries thought there could be an advantage in playing the USA off against the other. Friendlier relations with the USA would also lead to increased trade that benefited everyone.

SALT

▲ A nuclear Intercontinental Ballistic Missile (ICBM) is launched from a submarine

The most important task was to reduce the danger of a nuclear war. The process of détente started with discussions about limiting the growth of nuclear weapons. These discussions were called the SALT talks, Strategic Arms Limitation Treaty talks. Of course there had been talks and treaties before, but SALT I was a breakthrough. The USA promised to accept the right of the USSR to practise their Communist system. Nixon agreed to increase trade and other links with the USSR, 'There must be room in this world,' Nixon said, 'for two great nations with different systems to live together and work together.' The SALT I agreement of 1972 was an important step. America agreed to supply cheap grain to the USSR. Another source of Cold War tension had been Berlin (Chapters 9 and 12). The USA agreed to recognise the existence of East Germany and its Communist government as a sovereign nation. In return, the USSR and East Germany guaranteed the security of West Berlin.

Nixon and Soviet leader, Leonid Brezhnev sign the 1972 SALT I treaty. It helped bring about a new era of cooperation and détente.

USA and USSR: Important treaties, 1963-1980

1963 Nuclear Test Ban Treaty
USA, USSR, and Britain agreed not to test nuclear weapons in space, above ground and under water.

1968 Nuclear Weapons Non-proliferation Treaty
USA, USSR, and Britain agreed to stop the spread of nuclear weapons to nations that didn't already have them.

1972 Berlin Agreement
West Berlin security guaranteed; USA recognised East Germany

1972 SALT I (Strategic Arms Limitation Talks)
USA and USSR agreed to limit their nuclear weapons; not to test or deploy new ICBMs* and submarine launched missiles

1975 Helsinki Agreement
USA, USSR and various European nations agreed that all European borders be respected; East-West co-operation; respect for human rights.

1978 SALT II**
USA and USSR agreed to limit each country to 2,250 missile launchers and further limits on bombers.

*ICBM Intercontinental Ballistic Missile

** SALT II was not ratified, that is approved, by the US Senate. After Soviet troops invaded Afghanistan in 1979, President Carter told the Senate to put off approval of SALT II. As a further protest, Carter insisted that US athletes boycott the 1980 Olympic Games in Moscow. Carter called the Soviet invasion 'the gravest threat to world peace since World War II'.

1 What is meant by détente?
2 How can Source A be used to explain the need for détente?
3 What was meant by 'a diplomatic revolution'?
4 How did the treaties 1963-78 reduce the danger of war?

Nixon and China

Nixon's greatest and most surprising success came in his dealings with Communist China. Since 1949 the USA had had no relations with the Communist People's Republic of China. There was a trade embargo and American companies were not allowed to sell to or buy from China. The US Government forbade its citizens to visit China.

The Chinese leader, Mao Zedong, was strongly anti-American. China gave considerable support to the North Vietnamese in their war against the USA. Without that support the Americans might well have won the war. When he took office, the Chinese Communist Party described President Nixon as, 'a gangster wielding a blood-dripping butcher's knife'. In turn, throughout his career Nixon had criticised China and opposed any American trade or dealing with them. He always referred to them as 'Red China'.

In 1972, after secret meetings between Henry Kissinger and the Chinese Government, President Nixon announced that he was going to visit China. Americans were amazed. Nixon told them, 'I will undertake a journey for peace'. The newspapers used words like 'stunning', 'unbelievable', and 'incredible' to describe his announcement.

Henry Kissinger was always dashing between the world's capitals on behalf of President Nixon. It became known as 'shuttle diplomacy'.

▼

D 'Eureka'

In early July [1971], Kissinger flew off to Asia. On July 9, in Pakistan, the reporters accompanying him were told he had a stomach ache and would stay in bed. He went out of a back door and to the airport, where a Pakistani jet waited to fly him over the mountains into China, code name for his trip was Polo. If all went well, he had a code word to flash to Nixon when he returned to Pakistan. On July 11 a cable from Kissinger had arrived. It read 'Eureka'.

Historian Stephen Ambrose's account of Kissinger's secret visit to China in 1971

In February 1972 Americans watched their President visit China. They saw him visiting important Chinese landmarks, such as the Great Wall, which they had been forbidden to visit. Nixon said his trip to China 'is like going to the moon'. He said that his visit should be remembered with the words on the plaque left by the astronauts on the moon, 'We came in peace for all mankind'.

▼ President Nixon with Chinese Prime Minister Zhou Enlai

E Nixon's view

The most important decision that I made this year was the decision to open communications with China. I could do it where others could not. I believe that it will make a greater contribution to the next generation, to peace in the world, than anything else we have done. It was a difficult decision because it was a mixed bag as far as public reaction was concerned.

President Nixon in an interview with *Time* magazine, January 1972

There were several practical results from Nixon's trip. Steps were taken to start trade between China and the USA. Cultural, scientific, and sporting exchanges were set up. 'Liaison offices' were set up which were really unofficial embassies. Later, in 1979, the USA gave official diplomatic recognition to the People's Republic of China. Most important of all was the reduced hostility between the two countries. The chance of war was lessened. As a result of their President's trip, Americans of all walks of life adopted a more positive and tolerant approach to the Communist countries.

President Nixon's achievement in bringing about détente with the USSR and warmer relations with China marked the real beginning of the end of the Cold War. Nixon gained great personal prestige. In 1972 the influential news magazine, *Time*, made him their 'Man of the Year'.

Historians have argued that only Nixon could have achieved détente. Because he had attacked Communism all his political life he was able to convince anti-Communists that it was in America's best interest to have good relations with the great Communist powers.

F Nixon assessed (1)

Nixon's anti-Communist credentials were impeccable... had anyone but Nixon tried to promote détente, Nixon would have been the leading, and devastating critic, who would have rallied the right wing to kill the initiative.

Historian, Stephen Ambrose, writing about Nixon in 1989

G Nixon assessed (2)

He went to China. These simple words describe the most enduring achievement of Richard Nixon's presidency and America's most outstanding foreign policy initiative in the post-war period... It took his internationalist conviction, his uncompromising courage and the strange forces that shaped his character to pull it off... The United States was fortunate that, when opportunity called, Nixon was in the White House to answer it.

British politician, Jonathan Aitken, writing about Nixon in 1993

5 How would Americans have reacted to the news that their President was going to visit China?

6 Why did Kissinger's cable, Source D, say 'Eureka'?

7 Was it reasonable for Nixon to compare his visit to China with the moon landing?

8 List some of the benefits to China and the USA of Nixon's trip.

9 As the Editor of *Time* write a brief explanation of why Nixon should be 'Man of the Year'.

10 'Only as an anti-Communist could Nixon have recognised Red China'. Explain this statement.

17 Nixon and the Watergate affair

In 1972 *Time* magazine made President Richard Nixon their 'Man of the Year'. Two years later Nixon became the first ever President to resign from office. Nixon's disgrace and resignation resulted from the Watergate affair. Scandals involving politicians are not unusual. Watergate was the most serious scandal ever to affect the presidency. It created a constitutional crisis and undermined people's respect and confidence in their government.

The break-in at the Watergate

The Watergate complex is a large office building in Washington DC. In 1972 the Democratic Party had their headquarters in the Watergate. 1972 was election year and President Nixon, a Republican, was keen to be re-elected by a large majority. He knew that if he defeated the Democrat candidate by a large majority that he would be in a very strong position to get his way with Congress during the next four years.

Around midnight on 17 June 1972 five men wearing surgical gloves were caught by three policemen inside the Democratic Party Offices. They had forced their way in. Apparently, they were trying to place listening or 'bugging' devices inside the Democrats' office. Perhaps they were also looking for confidential documents. All of them worked for the Republican Committee for the Re-election of the President, usually known as CREEP. One of them, James McCord, was the Committee's security chief.

At first there was nothing to indicate just how serious this bungled break-in was, or the sensational consequences it would have. The Democrats alleged the 'break-in was a blatant act of political espionage'. The Republican Party and President Nixon, together with his White House staff, strongly denied any involvement in the break-in. Few people took the incident very seriously. One senior official described it as simply a 'caper'. Everyone, including the President, expected the whole matter to 'blow over'.

The break-in had no effect on the election. Throughout the campaign the Democrat candidate, George McGovern, complained bitterly about the 'dirty tricks' of the Nixon Administration. McGovern didn't stand a chance. President Nixon commanded great respect and support. Through his visits to the USSR and China he had brought a virtual end to the Cold War. He had withdrawn US ground troops from Vietnam. In 1968 Nixon had won only a very narrow victory. On 7 November 1972 Nixon defeated George McGovern by a landslide. It was the greatest victory of any Republican presidential candidate in history.

President Nixon and Vice President Agnew congratulate each other on their 1972 election success

A Nixon's election victories

1968	Nixon (Republican) 31,785,480 votes
	Humphrey (Democrat) 31,275,166 votes
1972	Nixon (Republican) 47,165,234 votes
	McGovern (Democrat) 29,170,774 votes

They [the Republicans] tried to place listening devices in my campaign office. They attempted to throw campaign schedules into disarray. They forged letters. They followed our families. They even plotted a disruption of their own Republican convention in Miami Beach so they could blame it on the Democrats... During 18 years in politics, I have never seen such efforts to poison the political dialogue. These Republican politicians have fouled the political atmosphere for all of us who see public service as a high calling.

The men who have ordered political sabotage, who have invaded our offices in the dead of the night – all of these men work for Mr Nixon. Most of them he hired himself. And their power comes from him alone. They act on his behalf, and they all accept his orders... And he has blocked any independent investigations.

George McGovern in a campaign speech just two weeks before the election.

The cover-up

There is no evidence that President Nixon knew about the Watergate break-in before it happened. But people working for him were directly involved and did know about it. When Nixon found out that some of his closest advisors were involved, he decided there should be a cover-up. John Dean, his lawyer, suggested a million dollars would be needed to keep the burglars quiet. Nixon told him, 'You'd better damn well get that done, but fast.' It was his use of presidential power to cover-up illegal actions by his staff that was Nixon's crime. The President tried to block investigations by the police, the Justice Department, and even the US Congress. Gradually the truth began to emerge. Newspapers and television were important in digging out and reporting the facts.

After the conviction of the five burglars, the US Senate decided to set up a special Committee to investigate the Watergate affair. One of the burglars had confessed that important men in the White House had been involved and that he had been offered a large amount of money to keep his mouth shut. The Committee hearings were shown on television. One witness, John Dean, changed sides and accused Nixon of obstructing justice. It was a sensational allegation but evidence was needed to back it up. Nixon went on television to tell the American people that he was entirely innocent of any wrongdoing.

The televised Senate Watergate hearings produced incredible accounts of Nixon's behaviour

I want the American people, I want you to know beyond the shadow of a doubt that during my terms as President, justice will be pursued fairly, fully, and impartially, no matter who is involved. This office is a sacred trust and I am determined to be worthy of that trust... We must maintain the integrity of the White House, and that integrity must be real, not transparent. There can be no whitewash at the White House.

President Nixon speaking on television, 30 April 1973

The Watergate tapes

In July 1973 an official who worked at the White House told the Senate Committee that since 1970 Nixon had recorded all his telephone conversations as well as the discussions that took place in the President's Oval Office. These tapes provided the evidence that Nixon had indeed been trying to cover-up the involvement of his staff in the Watergate burglary. All his denials had been untrue. Nixon had lied to the American people.

Nixon was forced to hand over 'secret' tape recordings of his private conversations in the presidential Oval Office.

Nixon tried desperately to stop the Committee getting their hands on his private conversations. But in the end he had to. There were increasing demands for his impeachment. That is the method by which a President can be removed from office. Even so, investigators studying the tapes discovered that a key section lasting 18 minutes was missing from a conversation about Watergate. Nixon blamed his secretary for accidentally erasing it. But experts decided that the erasure had been deliberate.

The taped conversations shocked people. They were surprised to learn that in the privacy of his office he frequently used foul language. But it was the tone of the conversations that disgusted people. Some people thought he sounded more like a gangster plotting how to get away with criminal activity. Nixon seemed to think that he didn't have to obey the laws that everyone else did. 'When the President does it,' he later told a TV interviewer, 'that means it is not illegal.' Anger grew and support for the President collapsed. Critics changed the presidential anthem 'Hail to the Chief' to 'Jail to the Chief'. Nixon faced the real possibility of not only being impeached but also of going to prison.

Resignation

On 8 August 1974 President Nixon resigned. He is the only President ever to have resigned. In a quite unrelated scandal in 1973 his Vice President, Spiro Agnew, had also resigned. A month after Nixon's resignation the new President, Gerald Ford, granted Nixon a pardon so that he could not be prosecuted. Most people thought that Nixon and Ford had done a deal. Nixon agreed to resign in return for the pardon. President Ford denied it: 'There was no deal'.

Nixon struggled desperately to hang on as public demands grew that he be removed from office

D Resignation

In all the decisions I have made in my public life. I have always tried to do what was best for the Nation. Throughout the long and difficult period of Watergate, I have felt it was my duty to persevere, to make every possible effort to complete the term of office to which you elected me.

I have never been a quitter. To leave office before my term is completed is abhorrent to every instinct in my body. But as President, I must put the interest of America first. America needs a full-time President... To continue to fight through the months ahead for my personal vindication would almost totally absorb the time and attention of both the President and the Congress in a period when our entire focus should be on the great issue of peace abroad and prosperity at home. Therefore, I shall resign the presidency, effective at noon tomorrow.

President Nixon's televised resignation speech, 8 August 1974

Totally humiliated, Richard Nixon resigned and made an emotional farewell to his White House staff

E 'Nightmare is over'

Our long national nightmare is over. Our Constitution works. Our great Republic is a government of laws and not of men.

The words of Gerald Ford on becoming President after Watergate

 Gerald Ford took the oath of office after Richard Nixon's resignation.

F Nixon on Watergate

What happened in Watergate was wrong. In retrospect, while I was not involved in the decision to conduct the break-in, I should have set a higher standard for the conduct of the people who participated in my campaign and administration. I should have established a moral tone that would have made such actions unthinkable. I did not. I played by the rules of politics as I found them. Not taking a higher road than my predecessors and my adversaries was my central mistake. For that reason, I long ago accepted overall responsibility for the Watergate affair. What's more, I have paid, and am still paying, the price for it.

Richard Nixon writing in 1990

After Watergate

Watergate left many Americans disillusioned with their system of government. They felt let down. Respect for the presidency declined. It was argued that the President had too much power. Critics called it an 'imperial presidency' and they wanted new laws to curb presidential power. There is no doubt that people no longer have the confidence or respect for politicians and government that they used to have.

An atmosphere of distrust

> Richard Nixon set out to change the politics of the country... in the end he probably did more than any other President of either party to destroy public confidence in all politics. It will not be known for some time what the Nixon years have done to the presidency itself – how severely its power has been diminished. That the office of President has been tarnished in the public eye cannot be denied.

Jules Witcover in the *Washington Post*, August 1974

H Nixon's legacy

> Nixon's legacy for our politics is more serious. His character came to represent political character generally ... the real cancer was more than just the corruption of one Administration; it was the corruption of politics as a whole in the mind of a generation. President Clinton is suffering from it. He and every other politician in America are still reaping the bitter harvest of Nixon's career, in distrust of leaders, lack of respect for institutions, and cynicism about public service. We don't have Dick Nixon to kick around anymore, but he'll be kicking us and our politics.

John Alter in *Newsweek* magazine after Nixon's death in 1994

I Public opinion

Do you trust the US Government 'most of the time'?		
1958	57%	Yes
1974	14%	Yes
1994	19%	Yes

Nixon and Agnew's behaviour inflicted a great blow to the presidency. For more than forty years the power and authority of the President had grown. That meant that the other branches of government, both the Supreme Court and the Congress, found it impossible to limit what the President did. But after the abuses of presidential power shown by Watergate there was a new determination to enforce limits on what a President could do. Perhaps the most important was a strengthened *Freedom of Information Act*. This makes it easier for citizen's to obtain official documents and so find out what their government is up to.

Increase in presidential staff
(Source: Congressional Research Service.)

	1954	1971
Presidential advisers	25	45
White House Staff	266	600
Executive Office Staff	1175	5395

Watergate and the 1976 Election

Watergate cast a shadow over the 1976 presidential election. There was widespread disillusionment with all politicians. The Democrats chose as their candidate a peanut farmer from the southern state of Georgia, Jimmy Carter. At first people spoke of him as 'Jimmy who?'. Outside of Georgia he was unknown. Because he was not a national political figure, he found it easier to win people's trust. He promised, 'I will never lie to you'.

K 'Our national nightmare'

Our national nightmare began with the assassination of Robert Kennedy, and of Martin Luther King... We watched the widespread opposition to the war in Vietnam, and the division and bitterness that war caused, and the violence in Chicago in 1968, and the invasion of Cambodia, and the shootings at Kent State, and revelations of official lying and spying and bugging, the resignations in disgrace of both a President and a Vice President... No other generation in American history has ever been subjected to such a battering as this.

Jimmy Carter, a campaign speech in 1976

L Carter's election victory

Carter (Democrat) 40,828,929 votes
Ford (Republican) 39,148,940 votes

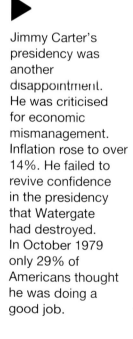

Jimmy Carter's presidency was another disappointment. He was criticised for economic mismanagement. Inflation rose to over 14%. He failed to revive confidence in the presidency that Watergate had destroyed. In October 1979 only 29% of Americans thought he was doing a good job.

Carter tried to restore Americans' faith in their government. His administration included more black Americans and women than ever before. But Carter only served one term. Serious economic problems with rising inflation and an oil crisis which led to high petrol prices lost him support. His failure to gain the release of US hostages held in Iran sealed his defeat in 1980.

1 You are working for Nixon's re-election, put the case for and against breaking into the offices of the Democratic Party.
2 Why was the Watergate break-in not taken very seriously at first?
3 Why did McGovern make the speech, Source B?
4 What did Nixon hope to achieve by his speech, Source C?
5 Do the facts support or contradict what Nixon said in Source C?
6 Was Nixon foolish to tape his private conversations?
7 Does Nixon admit wrongdoing in Source D?
8 How would these people react to Source D?
   (a) George McGovern
   (b) a 1972 Nixon voter.
9 Explain the point Gerald Ford makes in Source E?
10 How does Nixon try to explain his actions in Source F?
11 What problems do we face when we use sources such as Source F?
12 Which three questions would you have liked to ask Nixon about the Watergate affair?
13 What answers might he have given to your questions?
14 How would Americans have reacted to Watergate?
15 How would Source J have been used by those who wanted to limit the power of the President?
16 Richard Nixon died in 1994. Using Chapters 14–17 write an obituary of President Nixon.
17 Do you think Jimmy Carter's election victory was helped by Watergate?
18 Was it an exaggeration to describe Americans in the 1960s and 1970s as having been 'subjected to such a battering', Source K?

Essay:
i Explain why the Watergate affair did not 'blow over'.
ii What problems and what progress did America experience 1960–1980?

Index